Philanthropy and Public Policy

FRANK G. DICKINSON, *Editor*

A15021 029660

Conference on Philanthropy
Sponsored by
National Bureau of Economic Research
and
Merrill Center for Economics

ASU WEST LIBRARY
HV
25
.C7
1961
West

NATIONAL BUREAU OF ECONOMIC RESEARCH
1962

Copyright © 1962 by
National Bureau of Economic Research, Inc.
261 Madison Avenue, New York 16, N. Y.
All Rights Reserved
LIBRARY OF CONGRESS CATALOG CARD NUMBER: 62-20569
Price: $2.50
Printed in the United States of America

NATIONAL BUREAU OF ECONOMIC RESEARCH
1962

OFFICERS

Harold M. Groves, *Chairman*
Arthur F. Burns, *President*
Albert J. Hettinger, Jr., *Vice President*
Donald B. Woodward, *Treasurer*
Solomon Fabricant, *Director of Research*
Geoffrey H. Moore, *Associate Director of Research*
Hal B. Lary, *Associate Director of Research*
William J. Carson, *Executive Director*

DIRECTORS AT LARGE

Robert B. Anderson, *New York City*
Wallace J. Campbell, *Nationwide Insurance*
Erwin D. Canham, *Christian Science Monitor*
Solomon Fabricant, *New York University*
Marion B. Folsom, *Eastman Kodak Company*
Crawford H. Greenewalt, *E. I. du Pont de Nemours & Company*
Gabriel Hauge, *Manufacturers Hanover Trust Company*
A. J. Hayes, *International Association of Machinists*
Albert J. Hettinger, Jr., *Lazard Frères and Company*
Nicholas Kelley, *Kelley Drye Newhall Maginnes & Warren*
H. W. Laidler, *League for Industrial Democracy*
George B. Roberts, *Larchmont, New York*
Harry Scherman, *Book-of-the-Month Club*
Boris Shishkin, *American Federation of Labor and Congress of Industrial Organizations*
George Soule, *South Kent, Connecticut*
Joseph H. Willits, *Armonk, New York*
Donald B. Woodward, *A. W. Jones and Company*
Theodore O. Yntema, *Ford Motor Company*

DIRECTORS BY UNIVERSITY APPOINTMENT

V. W. Bladen, *Toronto*
Arthur F. Burns, *Columbia*
Lester V. Chandler, *Princeton*
Melvin G. de Chazeau, *Cornell*
Frank W. Fetter, *Northwestern*
R. A. Gordon, *California*
Harold M. Groves, *Wisconsin*
Gottfried Haberler, *Harvard*
Walter W. Heller, *Minnesota*
Maurice W. Lee, *North Carolina*
Lloyd G. Reynolds, *Yale*
Paul A. Samuelson, *Massachusetts Institute of Technology*
Theodore W. Schultz, *Chicago*
Willis J. Winn, *Pennsylvania*

DIRECTORS BY APPOINTMENT OF OTHER ORGANIZATIONS

Percival F. Brundage, *American Institute of Certified Public Accountants*
Harold G. Halcrow, *American Farm Economic Association*
Theodore V. Houser, *Committee for Economic Development*
S. H. Ruttenberg, *American Federation of Labor and Congress of Industrial Organizations*
Murray Shields, *American Management Association*
Willard L. Thorp, *American Economic Association*
W. Allen Wallis, *American Statistical Association*
Harold F. Williamson, *Economic History Association*

DIRECTORS EMERITI

Shepard Morgan, *Norfolk, Connecticut*
N. I. Stone, *New York City*

RELATION OF NATIONAL BUREAU DIRECTORS TO PUBLICATIONS REPORTING CONFERENCE PROCEEDINGS

Since the present volume is a record of conference proceedings, it has been exempted from the rules governing submission of manuscripts to, and critical review by, the Board of Directors of the National Bureau. It has, however, been reviewed and accepted for publication by the Director of Research.

(Resolution adopted July 6, 1948, as revised November 21, 1949)

Participants in Conference on Philanthropy

F. Emerson Andrews, *The Foundation Library Center*
Vaughn D. Bornet, *The RAND Corporation*
Kenneth E. Boulding, *University of Michigan*
James M. Buchanan, *University of Virginia*
Merle Curti, *University of Wisconsin*
Frank G. Dickinson, *National Bureau of Economic Research*
Richard Eells, *General Electric Company*
Solomon Fabricant, *National Bureau of Economic Research*
Leigh Gerdine, *Washington University*
Eli Ginzberg, *Columbia University*
Robert H. Hamlin, *Harvard University*
Covington Hardee, *Clark, Carr & Ellis, New York City*
Edward J. Kane, *Princeton University*
Thomas Karter, *Department of Health, Education, and Welfare*
Herbert E. Klarman, *Hospital Council of Greater New York*
Robert H. MacRae, *Welfare Council of Metropolitan Chicago*
James N. Morgan, *University of Michigan*
Natalie Naylor, *National Bureau of Economic Research*
Ralph L. Nelson, *National Bureau of Economic Research*
Ray M. Peterson, *The Equitable Life Assurance Society of the United States*
Eustace Seligman, *Sullivan and Cromwell, New York City*
Maud Seligman, *New York City*

Clarice Brows Thorp, *The Merrill Center for Economics*
Willard L. Thorp, *Amherst College*
W. Homer Turner, *U.S. Steel Foundation, Inc.*
William S. Vickrey, *Columbia University*
Colston E. Warne, *Amherst College*
John H. Watson, III, *National Industrial Conference Board*
W. Rulon Williamson, *Washington, D. C.*
Joseph H. Willits, *Armonk, New York*
Donald Young, *Russell Sage Foundation*

Contents

Preface

The National Bureau of Economic Research in cooperation with the Merrill Center for Economics held a conference on philanthropy at the Merrill Center, Southampton, Long Island, from June 26 through June 30, 1961; the conference was continued by the latter through July 7. Willard L. Thorp, Director of the Merrill Center, was chairman of the eighteen sessions held.

The conference was organized to examine economic aspects of philanthropy with particular attention to public policy. The scope of the conference is indicated in the following suggestive questions which were included in a statement sent in advance to the conferees:

> What is the appropriate "division of labor" among government, the market, and private philanthropy, in meeting human needs most effectively? Have the appropriate lines of division changed; do they continue to change; in what direction should they change? Should government continue to subsidize (or encourage) private philanthropy through the various provisions of the tax system (for example, tax exemption of property and of income; inclusion of philanthropic contributions among deductions for personal and corporate tax purposes)? Should government expand or contract its direct support, or alter the ways in which it directly supports private philanthropy? What of the respective roles of the federal, state and local governments? Should philanthropy, for purposes of governmental support, be redefined in any way? In what directions should private philanthropy concentrate its efforts, taking account of past and prospective expansion of govern-

mental activities and of market developments (private insurance, etc.)? What media of giving should be favored by private givers?

Five papers prepared for the conference and two earlier papers (by Fabricant and Dickinson) were sent to the conferees for use as background materials, but not for formal discussion at the conference. One of these, "Voluntarism in America—Attitudes and Behavior," by James N. Morgan, presenting data on contributions to church, charity, and other individuals as well as attitudes toward interfamily support, will be largely printed in *Income and Welfare in the United States,* to be published by McGraw-Hill in 1962. After the conference, Willard L. Thorp prepared a paper entitled "The Poor Law Revisited." His paper, the other six papers, and my brief digest of what was said at the conference comprise this volume.

Special acknowledgment is made to Amherst College and the Merrill Center for Economics, and especially to the Director and Assistant Director of the Center, Willard L. Thorp and Clarice Brows Thorp, for cosponsoring the conference and for permitting us to utilize the discussions of both weeks; to the Russell Sage Foundation which aided in financing the conference; to the authors of the papers and the participants in the conference; and to Edward J. Kane, who served as rapporteur and whose mimeographed summaries of the individual sessions proved helpful. The preparation of the volume was greatly aided also by the extensive notes taken at each session by Natalie Naylor. H. Irving Forman drew the charts.

It is our hope that these papers will illuminate this ill-defined area of our economy and stimulate economists and others to delve much deeper into a dynamic subject which is not bounded by market forces.

FRANK G. DICKINSON

Northern Illinois University
DeKalb, Illinois

Philanthropy and Public Policy

An Economist's View of Philanthropy

SOLOMON FABRICANT
National Bureau of Economic Research and New York University

OF THE many aspects of philanthropy that attract the economist's attention, I shall point to three. One relates to the place of philanthropy in economic life; the second, to the remarkable acceleration that our generation has seen in the use of government and market to meet or obviate philanthropic-type needs; the third, to the causes that have kept private philanthropic giving rising with the nation's income, despite this development.

Let me mention immediately that I feel better able to raise questions than to answer them. The subject is complex. To take a broad view of philanthropy—and this is my objective—means to look at the entire social organization, to consider its moral as well as its economic roots, and to ask how society has responded to the stresses of technological and other change. But perhaps the best way to stir up questions is to be positive. I shall try.

Philanthropy, according to the dictionary, means "love towards mankind; practical benevolence towards man in general; the disposition to promote the well-being of one's fellow-men." If this is what we mean

NOTE: The author is indebted to Dr. Frank G. Dickinson and Dr. Ralph L. Nelson, of the National Bureau of Economic Research, for most of the estimates cited. The studies by Drs. Dickinson and Nelson are being financed by grants from the Russell Sage Foundation. Use was made also of the chapter on philanthropic contributions in Professor C. Harry Kahn's *Personal Deductions in the Federal Income Tax*, published for the National Bureau in 1960 by Princeton University Press.

[Reprinted from *Proceedings of the American Philosophical Society*, Vol. 105, No. 2, April 1961.]

by philanthropy, then philanthropy is spread far wider through economic life than most people will see at first sight. There is a touch of philanthropy in many of our actions. Of course, there is more philanthropy in the motivation of some of the things we do, and less—even none—in others. But philanthropy is more universal than is generally supposed. We tend to underestimate its role.

For this, one reason is inadequacy of statistics. When we ask how important philanthropy is in economic life, we stumble over poor information. Few of us would want to let our definition of philanthropic purposes and philanthropic giving be determined by the regulations of the Commissioner of Internal Revenue. These permit deduction for tax purposes of contributions to organizations, but not to individuals—outside as well as inside the family circle, strangers as well as friends. Contributions to organizations set up in the United States are deductible, but not contributions to organizations set up under foreign laws. Contributions to churches and veterans' organizations are deductible, but not those to political parties or propaganda organizations. Yet we tend to slip into a definition determined by the tax regulations. The available statistical information is largely confined to income tax data—how can we supplement these data? An independent definition is difficult—what should we add to the Commissioner's list, what subtract, and how support our changes? And to the extent that it influences the organization and direction of giving, the tax code justifies concentration on the deductible items. Statisticians are aware of the limitations of estimates, based largely on tax data, that current philanthropic giving equals 2 or 3 per cent of the nation's total income, but find it easy to forget the limitations. The public often is not even aware of them. Inclusion of philanthropic contributions to individuals and institutions not now on the Commissioner's approved list—even with allowance for overstatements on tax returns—might almost double the percentage.

Another reason why philanthropy is underestimated is that we usually concentrate on giving in a narrow sense. We tend to forget that to forego income also is to give. Thus, the tax code permits the deduction, on tax returns, of contributions in cash or property, but not of contributions in the form of personal services or (in large part) of the services of property. Nobody keeps books on housewives' or even corporate officials' time spent in philanthropic activities, but such contributions must make up a substantial sum. If we were bold enough to make an estimate, we would have to add it not only to philanthropic giving, but also to national income, which does not include such "imputed" items. But the former would be raised proportionately more than the latter, and the ratio of philanthropic giving to income would be pushed up significantly.

Every economist has in mind also a less obvious sense in which philanthropy may be broader and its role larger than any ordinary figures on philanthropic giving could suggest. The clergyman or scientist who accepts an income lower than he could obtain in another respectable calling, because he prefers to occupy himself with work deemed to be of greater social value, also is making a philanthropic contribution. It is very similar to the contribution of time and money made by others in support of church or research institute.

How much there is of this sort of giving is a matter of guesswork. I suspect there is a good deal of it. Indeed, is there not something like it in almost every activity of economic life, when we temper our search for personal advantage with some regard for the welfare, sensibilities and opinions of our fellowmen? It is there in lesser degree and it is less calculated than in the choice of an occupation, but I do not believe it is negligible. No one is philosopher enough to disentangle the motives involved in restraining one's passions and one's selfishness. No one is able to decide how much of this restraint is to be credited to what is, in a literal sense, true philanthropy, how much to a long-run assessment of one's personal advantage, and how much merely to keeping within the law. However, if even a fraction of this kind of "giving" to society at large belongs in the realm of philanthropy, it is important to our assessment. For decent conduct pays to society as a whole large returns, one form of which is a higher level of national income than would be possible otherwise. Underdeveloped countries are learning that in their rush to reach desired levels of economic efficiency time must be taken to develop the kind of business ethics, respect for the law, and treatment of strangers that keep a modern industrial society productive. Widening of the concept of family loyalty and tribal brotherhood to include love of man "in general" is a necessary part of the process of economic development.

I have just said that no one is able to disentangle motives, and I cannot pretend to do so myself. But—this is a third reason why we tend to underestimate philanthropy—should we ignore the philanthropic element that is woven also into our "selfish" motives? The desire to keep within the law is not entirely a wish to avoid confinement or a money fine. The fear and shame of violating the law is a reflection, in part, of one's regard for the welfare, sensibilities and opinions of our fellowmen. Similarly, the acceptance of a lower rate of pay than one could obtain in another occupation, because one likes to do basic research or social work, is not only a response to one's "likes." Why do people "like" to add to knowledge or to work with people needing help? It is easy to recognize the selfish element in philanthropic giving. Should we not also recognize the philanthropic element in our selfish actions—and the importance of maintaining and strengthening this element? I do not think we can really understand the operations of a market economy if we think of it as populated by the vulgar conception of the economic man. The inhabitant of the economist's economy is a civilized person.

But to say that philanthropy is a necessary condition of social existence is not to say that philanthropy—love of man in general—is a sufficient condition of social existence, or that it is the major force of economic life. We are sinners more than saints. It is all too evident that love of man in general, though it influences a great deal of behavior, is in limited supply, and is limited therefore in its role in the economic and other aspects of life.

Perhaps an analogy will clarify my point. It is one thing to have the habit of following the written and unwritten rules of the game, even when the umpire is not looking and even when the rules have been altered in a direction of which one does not approve. It is quite another thing to treat one's opponent more gently than the rules require. I have been underscoring the philanthropic contribution of the first, not of the second. Indeed, I hasten to add that the strength of the philanthropic motive, and the success with which it can be called upon in the day-to-day business of life, is sometimes exaggerated. This is evident when special appeals are made to businessmen not to profiteer, to consumers to avoid selfish accumulation in anticipation of price rise, to employers and trade unions to compose their differences in the light of the public good. Study of human behavior has not made economists optimistic about men's response to such appeals. In Adam Smith's words:

> It is not from the benevolence of the butcher, the brewer, or the baker, that we expect our dinner, but from their regard to their own interest. We address ourselves, not to their humanity but to their self-love, and never talk to them of our own necessities but of their own advantages.

Economists might wish it to be otherwise, but their analysis stops them from putting much stock in philanthropy as a large means of getting the ordinary work of the economy done.

To continue with the analogy, progress has been made by joining together to tighten, and teaching ourselves to follow, the rules that govern us all, not from depending upon the individual player to rise above them.

Progress has been made also by joining together in collective action, through government, to promote the well-being of our fellowmen. During the past three decades the trend in this direction has been accelerated, and the rise of this and other ways to meet or anticipate philanthropic-type needs constitutes the subject of my second main observation.

One could slur over the difference between an individual's voluntary gift to the poor widow and the governmental assistance that is financed by taxation, and consider them both to be philanthropy. As we all know, the pressures to give "voluntarily" come from without as well as within, and the difference is therefore sharp only in a legal sense. But the term philanthropy may be, and usually is, restricted to voluntary payments by individuals and private corporations; governmental payments are then thought of as a substitute for these.

Whatever the terminology, however, one can hardly understand the role of philanthropy without a look at what government does. Whatever the terminology, also, it is desirable to make a distinction between private and governmental giving. Since government provides many free services and writes checks for many purposes, there will be obvious questions on what to include in governmental giving—whether, for example, to count not only payments to unfortunates, but also payments to persons blanketed into the Social Security system at a ripe old age; not only disaster relief to farmers, but also payments under the Agricultural Adjustment programs; not only domestic, but also foreign aid; not only cash payments to libraries and museums, but also the annual value of their exemption from property and income taxes. But while there will be differences of opinion about the purpose and magnitude of many individual items, by any reasonable criteria the aggregate of private and governmental philanthropy bulks large. A preliminary estimate, which includes governmental items some people would exclude and excludes items some would include, reached in 1958 something over a seventh of the national income.

My examples point also to some of the directions taken by governmental philanthropy since the 1920's. The story is one of more governmental operation of the institutions that provide philanthropic services, of more philanthropic payments by government—both to persons and to privately run institutions in support of the philanthropic services they provide, and of more governmental support in the form of taxes foregone.

A word needs to be said also about a parallel development in the marketplace. It was almost thirty years ago that the National Bureau published Pierce Williams' *The Purchase of Medical Care through Fixed Periodic Payment.* What has happened since in this and other market provision for meeting the needs of medical care (such as Blue Cross), of support in old age (such as private pension systems), and of still other "philanthropic-type" demands, constitutes another strand in the developments we are viewing.

To still another series of changes attention must be drawn in any broad view of philanthropy. Emerson Andrews has recalled to students of philanthropy Maimonides' words that the highest degree in the duty of charity, "the most meritorious of all, is to anticipate charity, by preventing poverty. . . . This is the highest step and the summit of charity's golden ladder." That in some major respects we are reaching, or reaching for, this step is the significance of numerous developments. In the governmental sector we now have an employment policy, for example, and we continue to improve public health measures. In the private sector, there have been successful efforts to reduce the accident rate, and to discover new methods of medical treatment. Most important has been a speedier increase in the nation's productivity than earlier generations enjoyed, and thus in the real income available to each family. This kind of "substitution" for philanthropy has always been a major goal of much of man's efforts.

The direction and general character of the various developments I have outlined are fairly clear. So, too, are their causes. Some are natural results of free enterprise: it pays individuals to invent better things or better ways to do things. Another set of developments may be seen as the fruit of earlier philanthropic investment in research. A major factor has been the rise of governmental activity in response to better knowledge of the sources of poverty, higher incomes, raised standards of well-being, and the working of the democratic process. This is a very large subject, and I shall merely mention that there must have been much interaction among the factors involved. Thus, the rise of government and along with it the imposition of a heavy progressive income tax has encouraged the development of private pensions and other fringe benefits and has directly affected the incentives to give for philanthropic purposes—which brings me on to my third main observation.

The figures that are being gathered together in a National Bureau study of philanthropy indicate that private philanthropic giving, as ordinarily defined, has more than kept pace with the national income or product. Indeed, a very preliminary estimate suggests a rise, in the ratio of private philanthropic giving to national income, from about 2 per cent in 1929 to between 2 and 3 per cent in 1958. But even if not so sharply upward, it is remarkable to find a rise in a period in which governmental and market activities and devices to take care of philanthropic-type needs have expanded so much. What is the explanation?

The reason is not to be found, I should say, in a relative rise of private giving for religious purposes—purposes that are not directly supported by government (except in a small way through tax exemption) or by the market. Indeed, philanthropic giving to religious organizations, which accounts for something like half of the total of private giving reported, has apparently risen somewhat less rapidly than private contributions for other purposes. Our question remains.

I would suggest, first, that there has been a shift from the kind of giving that is not covered by the statistics—giving by persons to other persons, and the giving of personal services and the services of property—to the kind of contributions that do get into the statistics. For this presumption, several reasons may be offered: government has taken over a very large share of the responsibility for the relief of unfortunates; the development of such market devices as Blue Cross has been rapid; contributions from persons to persons are not deductible under the income tax code and therefore now tend to be made indirectly through institutions; philanthropy has become professionalized in the sense that the scale of philanthropic institutions has grown, and the specialization that has taken place in this as in virtually all other economic and social activities has caused the displacement of voluntary work by professional service.

A second factor that comes quickly to mind is taxes. These are probably part of the explanation. Taxes can be very powerful influences on economic behavior, as economists would be among the first to admit. Yet it is easy to exaggerate their importance in the present case.

On the giving of the lower-income groups, where a very substantial part of all philanthropic giving originates, taxes may have only a small if any effect. The tax rates are low, and the standard deduction—permitted now for almost twenty years—has removed the tax incentive to make philanthropic contributions. It is worth mentioning that the introduction of the standard deduction in the early 1940's produced no obvious effect on the amount of philanthropic contributions reported on personal income tax returns.

As for the middle and upper income groups, income taxes reduce the cost—or "price"—of a philanthropic contribution by the marginal rate of tax. But they also cut the capacity to give by reducing income by the average rate of tax. The average is smaller than the marginal rate of tax, but comparison of the two rates is in itself insufficient to determine the net effect. Some economists, believing the effect on disposable income to be the more powerful, conclude that the high progressive income tax has tended to discourage contributions to philanthropic causes. It is true that the percentage of persons or families whose contribution to philanthropic causes comes near to the limit of tax deductibility is very low, and that the percentage of corporate profits contributed to philanthropic institutions, about 1 per cent, is much less than the maximum of 5 per cent that is allowed. But we know also that in some situations a contribution is costless; and there are estate taxes and other considerations—such as the wish to retain family control of a company—which influence giving. I expect that on net balance the tax system encourages philanthropic giving, but I find it difficult to believe that taxes constitute the dominant factor explaining the trend of philanthropic giving relative to the nation's income.

Real income per family is another factor in every economist's list. Such information as we have indicates that the higher the level of family income in any year (after a certain moderate income level has been reached), the higher is the ratio of philanthropic contribution to income or total expenditure. Inference from these "cross-sectional" data for a given year would suggest that the doubling of real income per family since the 1920's has been a powerful force pushing up the ratio of philanthropic giving to income. But there might well be technical flaws in such an inference, as economists have learned from studies of the "consumption function." Also, the data at hand fail to discriminate between the tax and the income effects. Further, it may not be the average level of income that, in any given situation, determines the percentage of income given for philanthropic purposes, but rather the distribution of income among families. Within the United States, it is interesting to observe, income inequality has declined since the 1920's, partly as a result of developments already mentioned. On the other hand, we may now be more keenly aware than before of the great disparity between incomes here and those in the rest of the world, and this would tend to work in the other direction. On the whole, I suspect that income, like taxes, has been less powerful in maintaining or raising private giving than quick inferences from available statistics might lead one to suppose.

Since we are speculating, let me add still another factor to the list. The increased knowledge and greater sense of collective rsponsibility, which have contributed to the rise of governmental activity in the philanthropic area, may have been accompanied by a heightened sense of the personal responsibility each of us feels for the welfare of his fellowmen. The professionalization of philanthropy and the rise of organized fund raising, to which reference has been made, may have assisted in this development. If it has taken place, it, too, has helped to maintain private giving. If my surmise is correct, there is here a sign —along with other signs, such as the changing attitude towards racial discrimination—of moral progress. But it would be very difficult to confirm the surmise without somehow measuring the contribution of all the other factors mentioned, a job still to be done. The possibility should be kept in mind that I see signs of moral progress only because I would like to do so.

We have been approaching, in this brief review, one of the fundamental questions that confronts every society. It is the question put sharply by Jeremy Bentham a hundred and fifty years ago, when he asked what should be the respective roles of government and of private enterprise—and we would distinguish, further, philanthropy—in advancing the common good? What ought to be done by government? What should be reserved to the people, pursuing their private interests or their philanthropic?

As did Bentham, we know—our national policies reveal the conviction—that each has its appropriate function and its special strength; that while government, market, and philanthropy are competitive, they are also complementary.

And we know, too, as did Bentham, that the optimum combination varies with the existing circumstances—with the stage of development of the society and of the capacities and habits of the people. When we look ahead, therefore, we can see further changes in the respective roles of government, market, and philanthropy in meeting the problems created by the continual change about us. But that private philanthropy will continue to play an essential role in our society—feeding and exercising and strengthening, with its teaching and its example, the spirit of brotherhood basic to social existence; using its independence of thought and its initiative and its "venture" capital to seek and discover and test new ideas and better ways to do things—of this we can have no doubt.

The Growth of Private and Public Philanthropy

FRANK G. DICKINSON
National Bureau of Economic Research and Northern Illinois University

Introduction

OURS is the first century in which long life for the many was achieved. The fear of living on into old age, especially penniless old age, has been one of the dominant social factors in changing the role of philanthropy in the American economy.

Dying old is the greatest triumph of the twentieth century; and that implies that it is probably the greatest triumph in man's history. I prefer the phrase, "dying old," because it is more realistic as a description of that triumph than to say that people now live much longer. Moreover, it avoids the inference that a certain percentage of all deaths can be prevented. Also, dying old implies that the function of the physician is to change the age and the cause of death, that birth is still a death sentence indefinitely suspended, and that the physician's task is to suspend the sentence a little longer.

Let us briefly review some of the salient mortality facts of the

NOTE: This paper is a mid-term report on a three-year study of The Changing Position of Philanthropy in the American Economy by the National Bureau of Economic Research under a grant from the Russell Sage Foundation. All the figures are tentative and subject to change. [Reprinted from Eastern States Health Education Conference, *Voluntary Action and the State,* New York, 1961, by permission of the New York Academy of Medicine.]

The views expressed are solely those of the author.

FIGURE 1

Expectation of Life at Birth in the United States
First Half and Second Half of 20th Century

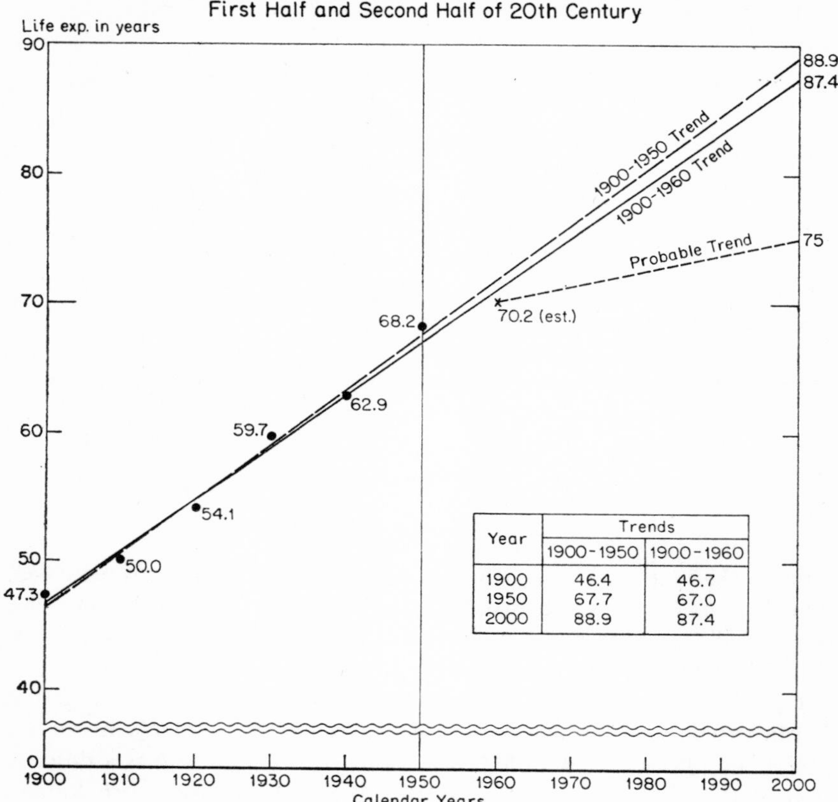

Year	Trends	
	1900-1950	1900-1960
1900	46.4	46.7
1950	67.7	67.0
2000	88.9	87.4

twentieth century. First, the expectation of life at birth has increased from 47.3 years in 1900 to 68.2 years in 1950, a gain of about 21 years in half a century, or slightly more than an average of four years a decade. Elsewhere I have shown reasons for believing that the expectation of life at birth might climb to 75 years in the year 2000.

Figure 1 gives the decade figures for expectation of life at birth from 1900 through 1950 (and 1960) and an extrapolated straight line trend. It indicates a value for the calendar year of 2000 of about 89 years.

I do not think that high level will be attained. I have also shown a dotted "most probable" line to 75 years in 2000. During the 1950's the gain has been less than two years. Apparently the life tables for 1959 to 1961 will be published late in 1962 by the National Office of Vital Statistics, or early in 1963. It is reasonably clear now, without having all the deaths of 1961 at hand, that the gain shown by the new life tables will be less than two years above the high level of 68.2 attained in 1950. I hope this forecast will be heeded. It could prevent some red faces among certain boastful leaders of the medical profession and the drug industry.

The prospect for the second half of this century is very, very different from the phenomenal and unique accomplishments of the first half of the century. Expectation of life at birth in 1950 could have been 75 years, instead of the 68.2, if there had been no deaths among persons under 53 years of age during 1949–1951. I don't want to quote an excess of statistics, but merely to leave the impression that when one studies philanthropy—which for the present we will define as "love of mankind"—during the past three decades, the imprint of the lengthening of life has been very great on that area of our economy. The impact on philanthropy of new health progress during the second half of our century should be far less than it was during the first half.

There are two other vital statistics to which I need to call your attention. The first is that the older half of the people dying in 1900 had lived at least 30 years, whereas the older half of the people dying in 1959 had lived at least 68.7 years. The other fact coming out of these statistics is that in 1900 about 24 per cent of all eligible voters, that is of all adults, were over 49 years of age; almost 38.5 per cent of the eligible voters in 1960 had lived at least half a century. These two facts reflect changes in birth rates and immigration in addition to mortality reductions.

A New Fear

I cannot end this introduction without bringing in some philosophical inferences which I think play a role in philanthropy, that is, love of mankind nurtured by religious teaching. One might ask why the modern child should fear God. A funeral sermon for a man of 69 (the median age of death in 1959) engenders gratitude, not fear—gratitude that God had allowed your late friend to complete his working lifetime, see his children attain middle age, and enjoy his grandchildren. Death at 30 years of age in 1900, the median age of death then, was a very different experience for the survivors. As the proverb has it, "The fear of God is the beginning of wisdom." But why should a child today fear God when he has been released from the fears that you and I knew as children? Why should the fear of death not be lessened when there is at least a possibility that a man with a test tube or a microscope tomorrow, or next week, or next month, will remove or greatly modify one of the important causes of death today and postpone our own death a few years? Small wonder that the Pilgrims at Plymouth feared God, for half of them died of disease during that first awful winter. Further pursuit of these speculations would carry me far beyond my main purpose. Merely let me say that dying old, by the process of eliminating the fear of early death from disease, has had, and will have, a tremendous influence on the spiritual development of the younger generations and those to follow. Let me hasten to note that medical and health progress can never be too rapid for me and my family. But I leave the further development of this point to the clergy of all faiths, with the suggestion that the most lasting result of dying old may be found in the realm of the human spirit. I am sure that the effects on the propensity to give are several.

I should like to conclude these introductory remarks with a question and a statistical observation. Is it reasonable to assume that the fear of living on into old age, indeed into penniless old age, has taken the place, so far as the study of philanthropy is concerned, of the fear of dying young at the turn of the century? Consider also the slowing down in the lengthening of life from 21 years in the first half to a notable increase of 7 years in the second half of our century.

Orphans

The reductions in mortality have materially reduced the probability that a newborn baby will lose one or both parents through death before the baby attains eighteen years of age. This is a rather complicated actuarial computation from mortality tables which I shall not try to deal with here. The reduction in the probability of becoming an orphan (single orphan or double orphan) has been very materially reduced; for babies born to young parents, by almost three fourths. The exact number of dollars that have been made unnecessary for the support of private and public philanthropic endeavors to take care of orphans cannot be precisely determined, but it is one of the brighter pictures in the field of philanthropy which reductions in mortality have produced.

The Growth of Private and Public Philanthropy

Our Concept of Philanthropy

The word philanthropy literally means "love of mankind." The starting point of this study of philanthropy must be a realization that love of mankind is the dominant idea of philanthropy. Although this doesn't help to circumscribe or indicate the limits of our investigation, I would say that anyone who makes a study of philanthropy dare not forget that this is the subject he is studying.

One always hesitates to try to define a concept as one can define a term. But one can describe a concept. At the present time I would say that what I mean by philanthropy is this: *giving money away to persons and institutions outside the family without a definite or immediate* quid pro quo, *for purposes traditionally considered philanthropic.* If we were in a position to measure philanthropy completely I would look for numbers which measure all types of transfer payments without a *quid pro quo,* excluding "transfers" between members of the family. The term, family, might well be used in the sense that it is used by the United States Bureau of Labor Statistics, the Office of Business Economics, and the Bureau of the Census to mean persons who are living together. But we shall never be able to pick up all the numbers that are needed to describe this ideal concept of philanthropy. I would like, for example, to include funds given by an uncle to a nephew or a niece for college tuition or for the expenses of attending college; but that is not possible.

Organization

Thus philanthropy involves a transfer payment without an immediate and definite *quid pro quo,* that is, no commodity or service is given in exchange. In a period of change attention should be given to activities traditionally considered to have been philanthropic. But perhaps the best way to describe the term philanthropy, as we are trying to use it in this three-year study is to describe the major divisions or parts of philanthropy.

In so doing, I shall shift back and forth from calendar to fiscal years. In general, we are covering the 31 years, 1929 through 1959; and expressing the trends in terms of Gross National Product (GNP). The straight "trend" lines shown on Figure 2 are not true trend lines but merely straight lines connecting the values for the first year and the terminal year of the period. The data on the diagram are prelim-

FIGURE 2

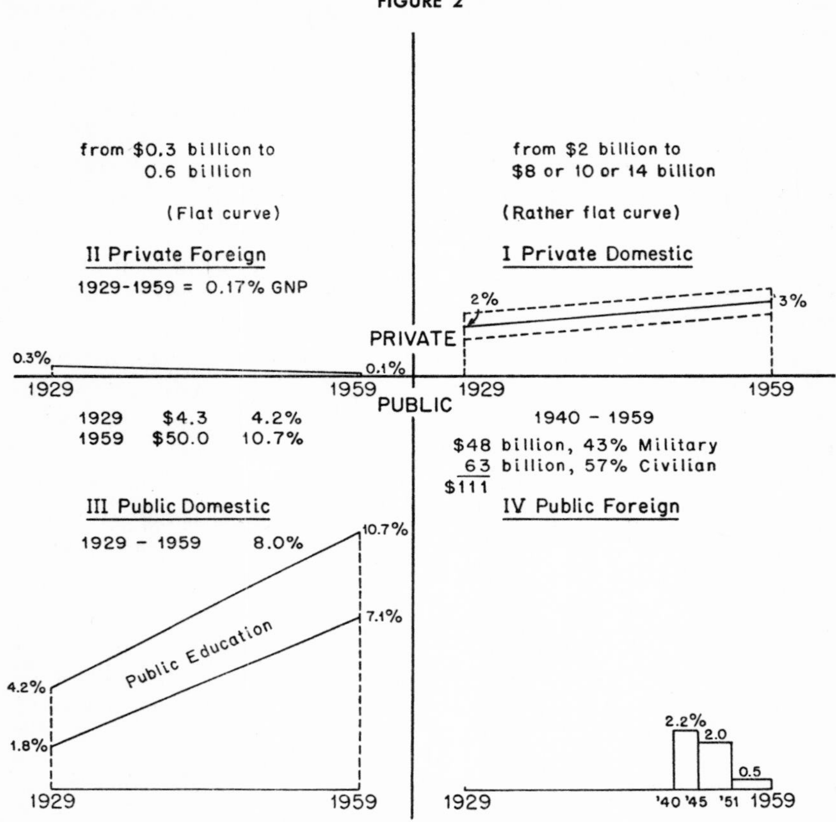

THE FOUR QUADRANTS OF PHILANTHROPY

(Preliminary Data)

Quadrants I and III will be stressed; II and IV will be given briefer treatment.

I. Giving by individuals and corporations to institutions and individuals.
II. Personal and institutional remittances abroad.
III. Social welfare expenditures, etc.
IV. Civilian aid.

Maximum % of GNP

	1929	1959
Q I	2—	3—
Q II	0.3	0.1
Q III	4.2	10.7
Q IV	—	0.3

(Final figure, say 1/10 of GNP)

"During this last half-century, American organizations—voluntary and governmental—have provided the margins of food, medicines, and clothing which saved the lives of 1,400,000,000 human beings, mostly women and children, who otherwise would have perished."—Herbert Hoover in *An American Epic*.

inary. Most of the figures are maximums or limits to guide us in our daily research.

Quadrants I and II are private philanthropy, domestic and foreign; Quadrants III and IV, below the horizontal line, are public philanthropy, domestic and foreign. Our "House of Philanthropy" will have four rooms. This diagram presents the fourfold organization of our study. I will describe briefly what we are finding about the extent of philanthropy. I shall express these billions of dollars mostly as percentages of GNP, i.e., the grand total of all commodities and services produced during the year. Unfortunately it does not include, for example, the housekeeping work of housewives as they are not paid wages. In general, we have selected the last three decades as the period for study although there are some years for which we either have no data or for which there should be no data. In this period GNP rose from 104 billion dollars in 1929 to 482 billion dollars in 1959.

Private Domestic Philanthropy

In 1959 the total giving for the items covered in Quadrant I, Private Domestic Philanthropy, was something *more* than 8 billion dollars. (The highest estimate we now have in our worksheets for institutions is 11 billion dollars.) Person-to-person giving is not recorded in the *Statistics of Income* because you cannot deduct it in computing your taxable income. Including the person-to-person giving—perhaps two-fifths of estimated giving by living donors—might produce a final grand total of 14 billion dollars in 1959. My comments on breakdowns of Quadrant I must be based largely on giving to institutions which can be deducted from income subject to personal income tax; nor can I go into detail about our figures for the additional item, person-to-person giving.

Of this sum of over 8 billion dollars, approximately three quarters was derived from individuals, and the balance from corporations, charitable bequests, endowments, and foundations. On the other hand, the functional distribution of private domestic philanthropy (Figure 2) was probably somewhat as follows: religion accounted for about half, welfare perhaps one sixth, and education, health and a variety of purposes accounted for the balance. For 1929, the beginning of our period, we are experiencing a good deal of difficulty in establishing an anchor. If I may pass over some difficult problems we have not yet solved, let me say that the figure was around 2 billion dollars in 1929, a year in which GNP was 104 billion dollars. In the sense that I suppose most people use the term "philanthropy," we are talking about a change from 2 billion dollars in 1929 to something more than 8 billion, perhaps 14 billion dollars in 1959. The amount of religious giving in 1929 was near three quarters of the total whereas now it is probably nearer one half.

The over-all observation about the first quadrant is that, as a proportion of GNP, there has not been very much change. We could fit all of our estimates into this band (on the diagram) slightly above and below 2 per cent in 1929 and 3 per cent in 1959. The predominant characteristic of the final trend line of Quadrant I will be rather flat. In other words, the philanthropic propensities of the American people as expressed in these common forms of private philanthropy—giving by individuals, corporations and business firms, charitable bequests and foundations for private domestic philanthropy—have little more than kept pace with GNP. Certainly we do not find in the first quadrant any very definite evidence that, in relation to GNP, the American people, despite their increasing affluence during these three decades, have become more philanthropically minded; or, to use a much earlier term, that the propensity to give has increased very much.[1]

Private Foreign Philanthropy

Now let me pass on to the second quadrant of the diagram (Figure 2); it, also, is private but it deals with giving specifically to persons and institutions in other countries. The grand total of philanthropy in Quadrant II is by far the smallest of the four quadrants. I shall not discuss some interesting fluctuations above and below the general level of one sixth of one per cent of GNP during the three decades.[2] (We have fitted a straight line trend to this period and found a negative slope value of 0.007 per cent.) Our conclusion, as far as this presentation is concerned, is that Quadrant II is rather steady and there has been a slight downward trend in the relationship to GNP. We plan to single out one of the agencies which may be typical of the several dozen agencies working in this area and describe it in some

[1] The use of other, smaller national aggregates for one or two of the quadrants, but not for the totals, will be discussed in our final report.

[2] The funds for Quadrant II originate in and are part of the total giving recorded in Quadrant I. Hence the amounts for Quadrant II are excluded from grand totals —of the other three quadrants only. The second quadrant is essential for the "where to" analysis.

detail. At the present time, I am leaning towards CARE as the agency. We shall describe rather briefly how CARE raises funds, how it manages fund-raising programs, the amounts that it gives and to what countries, and its procedures in giving in kind—giving surplus commodities rather than giving cash—to the needy peoples of various sections of the world.

I am interested especially in Quadrant II because we decided earlier in this study that we could not confine our attention to gifts from the people of the United States to other people and institutions in the United States, i.e., that we could not possibly confine our study to the national boundaries of the United States and give a clear-cut picture of the changing position of philanthropy in the American economy—the precise description of our three-year study project. Rather, it seemed clear that we would have to go beyond the boundaries of the United States in order to try to encompass the functioning of philanthropy in this dark corner of economic knowledge, and that the international aspects of philanthropy would have to be presented if we were to make any contribution to our system of national accounts.

Total Private Philanthropy

We close this part of our discussion with the observation that private philanthropy, considering domestic and foreign together (Figure 2, Quadrants I and II), has increased in the thirty-one years of the study perhaps a little faster than GNP. Certainly, so far as this diagram is concerned, we can say that above the line, despite the tremendous increase in all measures of economic growth—in national income, in personal income per capita, disposable income per capita, disposable income in terms of constant prices or other measures—and despite the fact that we have had an enormous improvement in the well-being of the American people in their standard of living, we fail to find *a marked increase in the propensity to give* which one might associate with the rising standard of living; an increasing propensity, I should have said, to give money away without a direct or immediate *quid pro quo* to traditional philanthropic endeavors. So we pass from the first and second quadrants into the third quadrant—from the bedroom and the kitchen to the large living room and the utility room of our "House of Philanthropy."

Public Philanthropy

In passing from the field of private philanthropy, both domestic and foreign, into the field of public (governmental) philanthropy, domestic and foreign, it might be worthwhile to stop a moment and consider again our concept. When I first started working on this three-year research project I read, of course, the National Bureau publications in this field. The first is a small volume by W. I. King, *Trends in Philanthropy,* published in 1928. It is a study of philanthropy in New Haven, Connecticut, 1900–1925. Dr. King listed seven *public* agencies of New Haven and West Haven in addition to the private agencies. Treatises on philanthropy in the 1920's considered both the local private and the local public agencies in trying to get a picture of the expenditures on philanthropy. In fact, we find in the literature published in the late 1920's frequent mention of both public and private philanthropy. I dare say that when most people use the term philanthropy today without a qualifying adjective they probably have private philanthropy in mind. I doubt that they did in the 1920's. The terms private and public have appeared in the literature often enough to warrant the use of both types in our present study.

The other general thought that has to be placed either before or after this discussion of the third and fourth quadrants (Figure 2) is that we can give money away without any immediate *quid pro quo* through agencies of government. Admittedly, private philanthropy is more voluntary. Yet I do not think there is anything voluntary about a gift of a corporation, say to an educational institution, from the standpoint of the shareholder. His opinion and consent are not asked about how much should be given and to whom. Of course, he can sell his shares of stock if he is not satisfied with the amounts the corporation gives or the amount that it gives for a particular purpose. Moreover, there is a considerable volume of discussion that we have encountered on whether or not it is proper for corporations to give when they are organized for the purpose of making profits for their shareholders.

In the ultimate sense we make purely voluntary decisions in relatively few cases of giving to the support of activities traditionally considered philanthropic. You can pass by the blind man or you can drop a coin in his tin cup. I presume this is one particular form of giving in which there is a very real degree of voluntarism. But many other gifts that we make involve some degree of pressure and a variety of considerations. Perhaps an examination of some of the forms of giving that we have called public philanthropy may bring this question into focus. At least, I hope at this stage that you do not close your mind to the possibility of giving money away through the processes of government itself. This applies particularly to types of activities that have been traditionally considered philanthropic. One would expect to find these types of government activities classified and compiled under social welfare expenditures. The boundaries of Quadrant III, Public Domestic Philanthropy, and the boundaries of social welfare expenditures are not the same. Social welfare expenditures would have been classified in other ways, e.g., state and local, if we were studying the first three decades of the twentieth century instead of the second three decades. Indeed, for an earlier period when there were not so many persons acting as individuals or as private or public officials giving away so much money to so many persons at home and abroad for so many purposes, our present concept of philanthropy might be too broad.

The Merriam Compilations

For our purposes, I shall first use the annual compilations of social welfare expenditures by Mrs. Ida C. Merriam, published in the *Social Security Bulletin* as Quadrant III (Figure 2). Later on, I shall discuss some additions and subtractions required to fit them into Quadrant III. Please note that the Merriam data are compilations of social welfare expenditures under public programs by fiscal years. As I have done in Quadrants I and II, I shall continue to stress what I think will be the *maximum* numbers that we shall use as our estimates in the study. In a number of instances, I am sure that our final totals will be lower. We cannot call attention here to every important item in her master table.

In the fiscal year of 1928–1929, according to Mrs. Merriam, 4.2 per cent of GNP of 101.6 billion dollars was devoted to her selected group of social welfare expenditures under public programs. If we were to remove from Mrs. Merriam's total the amount spent on public education—mostly nonfederal expenditures—the Quadrant III proportion of GNP would drop from 4.2 per cent to 1.8 per cent. The matter of inclusion or exclusion of expenditures for public education in Quadrant III takes on considerable importance. Her total for the fiscal year 1958–1959 is 10.7 per cent of GNP. In other words, using her grand totals *without modification* as coextensive with Quadrant III, we note a sharp upward rise, a steeply sloping upward curve if we just connect our points for 1929 and 1959—as shown in Figure 2. One observation is that in Quadrant III we are not contending with a flat curve but with a sharply rising curve. In her grand totals the proportion of GNP in 1959 was about 2.5 times the level of 1929, 10.7 per cent and 4.2 per cent. The exclusion of one of her major items, public expenditures for education, from Quadrant III indicates a three-fold increase from 1.8 per cent of GNP in 1929 to 7.1 per cent in 1959 for the subtotal; the curve for this subtotal (excluding only the large item for public education) is actually somewhat steeper. At this time I obviously cannot comment on the variations, the peaks, and valleys in the curve for her totals during the three decades; you can all well imagine that the amount spent on public aid (now Old Age Assistance, Aid to Dependent Children, etc.) was a peak portion of GNP in the Great Depression in the early 1930's. Reference now to data for specific years would be only a diversion from my presentation.

Old Age Assistance

One item, Old Age Assistance under the Social Security Act of 1935, has grown considerably; aid to the blind and to dependent children has also grown considerably since 1936. For many decades before the 1930's charitable support for these groups was provided by a variety of local private and local public agencies. We plan no adjustments in the Merriam totals for public assistance, as the concept coincides with our concept of Public Domestic Philanthropy. The poorhouse was, of course, already on its way out before the Social Security Act was passed in 1935. That act and the amendments thereto have produced most of the growth in Quadrant III; and most of the sharp upward trend that we do not observe in Quadrant II or Quadrant I.

Alternative Semantics

There are other semantic choices that can be made here. Some might prefer to think of Old Age Assistance provided through the Social Security Act, a federal-state program, as a substitute for philanthropy, or as a social device for making this particular form of private philanthropy largely unnecessary. That seems inherently awkward to me for the term supplement, or substitute, for private philanthropy doesn't seem to give us elbow room to answer the questions with which we are charged in this study: What has been the changing position of philanthropy in the American economy since 1929? It seems much easier to be very careful to use the terms "private philanthropy" and "public philanthropy" so that the distinction will be clear to the reader. Public philanthropy involves a flow of funds to areas traditionally considered philanthropic but directed through the process of government, through the election of our representatives, through their decisions to approve certain types and kinds of legislation, and through the opportunity to vote again for these same representatives who, on the whole, support the legislation wanted by citizens. In our free society we exercise our wills and we make our choices, thereby directing the changing position of philanthropy in the American economy. We give direction as voters and as citizens. We direct the flow of funds as individuals through our personal choices and through our private institutions into philanthropic endeavors. We approve transfer payments, for example, from the Young to the Old. By various routes we give money away without a specific *quid pro quo;* hence the four quadrants. If we were studying philanthropy in a closed society or in a communistic society, we would probably use a different concept.

Our Period of Study

The particular period of time that we have under observation demands a very broad, comprehensive concept of philanthropy, of giving our money away without an immediate *quid pro quo,* through private agencies, through private institutions with all manner of pressure being brought to bear on individuals; and the pressures on business units and corporations to give to this, that, and the other worthy cause; and through government. (Again, philanthropy is not circumscribed by the boundaries of the United States.) There are collective decisions that we make as citizens; for example, we vote school bonds to expand the educational facilities of a community long after our own children have grown up and passed beyond the school ages. I could discuss this question of voluntarism and compulsion in private and public philanthropy for a long time, and perhaps add very little. One friendly critic has urged me to exclude religious giving because the giver has a *quid pro quo,* i.e., he is seeking admission by St. Peter at the "pearly gates." He admitted, however, that the *quid pro quo* was neither definite nor immediate.

In summarizing about Quadrant III, I want to say that we have had a very sharp upward trend during these three decades in the proportion of GNP going to social welfare expenditure which, for the moment and for the moment only, I am accepting as a very rough first approximation of the types and forms of government expenditures which will go into this quadrant. Mrs. Merriam includes another huge item, veterans' welfare expenditures. I am inclined arbitrarily to set some fraction, say one third, of these welfare expenditures to be removed from Quadrant III, and to classify that annual amount under the aftercosts of war, not under philanthropy, however broadly defined.

Old Age, Survivors and Disability Insurance

We pass on to the item which is designed some day to take the place of the temporary Old Age Assistance program. I am referring now to Old Age, Survivors, and Disability Insurance (OASDI). This program involves puzzling questions for a student of philanthropy. It is my view that an examination of the record, particularly of the actuarial aspects of the record, will demonstrate that retired persons receiving Old Age and Survivors Insurance benefits are receiving sums of money which are at least 95 per cent "public charity," or transfer payments from the young to the old. In 1950 the percentage was slightly lower; possibly 94 per cent was "public charity." These old age pensions have not been prepaid. People have been blanketed into the program. All social security taxpayers collectively are paying only 42 per cent of what you would call the normal cost of the system; the children and the unborn must pay the deficit. In my opinion, the Social Security tax rate should be lower for young workers than for older employees. The value of the lifetime taxes of a young man just entering the system *plus* the value of his employers' taxes equals approximately 180 per cent of the value of the lifetime benefits under existing law. A further rise from 180 to 200 per cent would indicate trouble ahead.

Adjustments in Welfare Payments

The point I am trying to make here is that I am not quarreling with Mrs. Merriam's totals or compilations or what she does include or exclude. I am only saying our final totals for Quadrant III will not be as high under our more restricted definitions. Note that her grand total for fiscal 1958–1959 is 50 billion dollars or 10.7 per cent of GNP. I shall, for example, reduce her OASDI expenditure totals by 5 per cent, more or less, because that small proportion is not a transfer payment from the young to the old; it has been "prepaid"; it is not "public charity." For example, the entry in Quadrant III for OASDI for 1958–1959 would be 9.1 billion dollars, 5 per cent less than the 9.6 billion dollars in Mrs. Merriam's table. (For calendar 1959, the 10.3 billion dollars would be reduced 5 per cent to 9.8 billion dollars.) Nevertheless, it would still be the *largest amount* in any of the four quadrants. This is a major point in our study—the largest piece of furniture, the grand piano, if you please, in the largest room (the living room) in our "House of Philanthropy." Some may prefer to call this largest current item in philanthropy, broadly defined, a transfer payment from the rich and poor Young to the rich and poor Old. The term, "95 per cent public charity," may seem too strong, particularly to professional persons with no interest in actuarial matters. Nomenclature is always a problem in research.

On the other hand, I would express agreement with Mrs. Merriam in excluding a very important form of transfer payment that is being made and has been made for years starting with the Agricultural Adjustment Administration (AAA) for farmers. The payments to farmers were made under a changing system of production and price controls. While I grant that in the hands of the farmer these payments are welcome and can be used by the recipient more freely than some other types of welfare payment, I nevertheless could not see fit to include such payments in Public Domestic Philanthropy. In trying to draw the line on which expenditures of government shall be included under Public Domestic Philanthropy in Quadrant III we should be constrained by consideration of the fact that this changing farm program is primarily associated with our system of production. It was originated and has been continued as a program to control and to stimulate, particularly in time of war, the output of agricultural products. So I agree with Mrs. Merriam on the exclusion of farm aid.

We may, however, want to add expenditures (and facilities) for recreation. It seems to me that the provision for recreation for the public in Yosemite National Park or Yellowstone National Park and the consumption of the beauty of those places is quite as real as the utilities (the pleasures of consumption) enjoyed by the use of the knife, the fork, and the spoon. Our totals for Quadrant III, I repeat, are going to be lower than the totals one would obtain by merely taking the carefully developed annual estimates of Mrs. Merriam as they are published annually in the *Social Security Bulletin* and saying that these are coextensive with Quadrant III in our study of philanthropy. I appreciate that there is always an advantage in choosing a concept coextensive with some regularly published set of estimates which presumably will be regularly published in the future. But I don't think I should spend more time in going further into this subject of which social welfare expenditures should be included in Quadrant III, and which should be excluded. We have problems of semantics in Quadrant III, as well as in the other three quadrants. I cannot hope that every student will agree with us in every decision made to conform to our broad concept of philanthropy used in this three-year study of the changing position of philanthropy in the American economy during the past three decades.

Foreign Aid

We now turn to Quadrant IV (Figure 2), designated Public Foreign Philanthropy. Although some large numbers are involved in this quadrant, we should probably give it the least attention because we do not think it is within the scope of our study to follow foreign aid through to the country receiving it as to the manner in which the funds were actually spent on health, sanitation, transportation, communication, or education. We shall not investigate the manner in which each recipient country has used our foreign aid. Moreover, in this study of the changing position of philanthropy in the American economy we do not intend to attempt any essays on foreign aid or related aspects of international payments or international finance.

Between the Wars

As we enter Quadrant IV, we have to make some sharp compromises with the chronological pattern in Quadrants I, II and III for which I have been trying to give you some very quick estimates and some numbers for the period 1929–1959. The amount of public foreign aid between World War I and World War II, as I recall, was reported in one bulletin as a grand total of only 69 million dollars. You may recall the types and kinds of aid that have been given in cases of national disaster. We wish that we could go back before 1929 to World War I to get our bearings, to review the mixture of public and private philanthropy in the aid program directed by Herbert Hoover in Belgium. Foreign aid, 1914–1919, was a matter of borrowing, first from the people of the United States through private transactions which probably would not appear in any event in our totals, and second, by interallied loans which before and after the armistice totaled about 10 or 11 billion dollars. If we were to go through the 1920's in this study, we would, I suppose, be required to carry these accounts showing how the interallied debts were increased for nonpayment of interest and principal, the negotiations with Russia, negotiations over reparations with Germany and all of the complications of the Dawes plan, the Young plan, etc., leading up to the Hoover Moratorium of 1931. Despite our reluctant decision to say very little about World War I and the gap between World War I and 1940, I think it is worth noting that in some official compilations these interallied debts are still considered as obligations due the United States.

At this point, we shall modify the chronological pattern in this report. In Quadrant IV, for all practical purposes, we are talking not about 1929–1959, but about 1941–1959. During those two decades the grand total of foreign aid was divided roughly as follows: $48 billion military and $63 billion civilian, a total of $111 billion (Figure 2). That is a large sum of money. Our immediate interest is in the over-all division between military aid and civilian aid. The approximate breakdown here is 43 per cent military aid and 57 per cent civilian aid. Let us consider first a few broad questions about the cumulated aggregates.

Military Versus Civilian Aid

Was all of this expenditure of 111 billion dollars beyond the pale of philanthropy? Was it merely an aspect of national policy? Was military or civilian foreign aid (or both) during this troublesome period of 20 years giving money away without an immediate or definite *quid pro quo?* Was military foreign aid merely a substitute for spending the same amount on our own military establishment? Can one separate the military from the civilian? Admittedly, that separation is very difficult to make from the record itself; but I must not dwell on that point. Rather, from the standpoint of our broad concept of philanthropy (public and private), could one claim that the military aid was different from the civilian? Did not the billions of dollars put into military aid for any one country, any section of the world, provide funds by which the governments of those countries were able to improve the civilian economy in the sense that, if the support for the military establishment came from the United States, so many dollars, so to speak, were released for civilian use? I might say that this attitude—which I call indivisibility of military and civilian expenditures—is held by one of the persons in the United States Department of Commerce upon whom we have leaned rather heavily for data.

We have a number of choices here, perhaps none of them clean-cut. First, we could exclude Quadrant IV entirely and say that foreign aid in no way manifested the philanthropic propensities of the American people. I think that our study would be rather bitterly criticized if we were to say that none of this 111 billion dollars represented a philanthropic type of activity or intent on the part of the American people. Does it matter where the starving people were located or where they were living, within or outside the United States? Or that philanthropy is not involved if the United States government helps starving people during a war? I am not quite sure that we Americans have to shoulder the entire responsibility for the war and for the aftermath of the war. Certainly, to many people, we seemed to be giving away large sums of money.

Exclusion of Military Aid

For these and other reasons, I have tentatively decided to exclude from our Quadrant IV those expenditures for foreign aid which could be classified as military—43 per cent of the 111 billion dollars. This really is quite a hazardous line to draw when we know numerous instances of military supplies shipped to foreign countries which found their way into civilian uses, such as food for the military and gasoline for military equipment. Sometimes this diversion was a result of a very definite policy which had been established. We should not quarrel too much with Congressional semantics in placing military or civilian labels on these several programs. In Quadrant IV, I now plan to limit foreign aid to the 57 per cent labeled civilian aid, leaving the amounts spent for military aid during the nineteen years to be charged to some other sector of the national accounts such as the cost of aiding allies during and after wars. One suggestion made to us in this connection was that a reasonable division would be to exclude from Quadrant IV both the military and the civilian foreign aid during the war years, 1941–1945, and then to include both the military and civilian aid since the close of World War II. But this all-or-none treatment by war and postwar periods also seems to us less consistent with our pursuit of the changing position of philanthropy in the American economy than does the exclusion each year of military expenditures from Public Foreign Philanthropy so that what is counted in Quadrant IV is the sum of 63 billion dollars, the amount spent for civilian aid since 1941.

Obviously, trend lines from 1941 to 1959 have no special meaning. In 1959 civilian aid was 1.6 billion dollars or 0.34 per cent of GNP. In Figure 2, three short horizontal lines are shown in Quadrant IV: 2.2 per cent of GNP for 1941–45, 2.0 per cent for 1945–1951, and 0.5 per cent for 1951–1959. The three divisions of the postwar period and the three horizontal bars must suffice at this time.

For reasons stated and unstated, I am rather reluctant to present here a combined total of all four quadrants. But I will do so with two reservations: first, that our final numbers will be smaller in Quadrant III, and, second, that there may be some errors in computations which need to be corrected. So here is my over-all summary *at this time.* It is *not* the summary of our findings. I reserve the right to change every figure in this "mid-term" report.

Summary

1. During the 31 years covered by this study GNP was 6,700 billion dollars and the amount involved in philanthropy, using our broad definition, was probably of the order of 600 to 700 billion dollars.

2. Since the end of the 1920's the position of philanthropy—private and public, domestic and foreign—in the American economy has increased from *not more* than 7 per cent of GNP to *not more* than 15 per cent of GNP (see legend, Figure 2). The position of philanthropy in the American economy relative to GNP has approximately doubled in the last three decades. My best guess about our *final* figures is that philanthropy, private plus public, now accounts for at least one tenth (10 per cent) of GNP. *It did not in 1929.*

3. Let us break this thumbnail summary into quadrants. I am saying that the first quadrant today is about 3 per cent of GNP whereas at the end of the 1920's it was about 2 per cent. The second quadrant was 0.3 per cent in 1929 and 0.1 per cent in 1959.[3] For Public Domestic Philanthropy, using the social welfare compilations of Mrs. Merriam without any changes, the increase has been from 4.2 per cent of GNP to 10.7 per cent; as already noted, our total for Quadrant III will be less than 10.7 per cent. The fourth quadrant, Public Foreign Philanthropy, which was zero in 1929, is now of the order of one third of one per cent. Whatever the *final* percentages reported in our study may be, the grand total will not be below one tenth of GNP in 1959.

[3] See footnote 2.

Two very general observations based upon these provisional and unrefined data can be presented now as highly tentative answers to the question which we were assigned to investigate. First, if one examines the changing position of private philanthropy and limits himself to private philanthropy, one must conclude that the position of private philanthropy in terms of GNP had not materially changed since the end of the 1920's. Private philanthropy trends *understate* the generosity of our nation. Second, if one adds public philanthropy, as we have tried to sketch it here, one would say that the total of private and public philanthropy had increased considerably. *The economy now tithes.* The scriptural one tenth has been attained by a generous people! As stated in my preamble, the fear of outliving one's income has been one of the major conditioning forces.

One Economist's View of Philanthropy

William S. Vickrey
Columbia University

The theoretical economist's ideal model of the economic system is one in which each participating unit lives in its own compartment, completely isolated from all others except through the process of economic exchange. The market is such that prices are precisely determined by competitive forces as modified by taxes and other well-defined and specifically legislated provisions. Within these bounds each economic unit acts only in terms of its own direct interest, trusting in an unseen hand to bring harmony out of conflicting interests. But such a pure competitive economic system, even if it could be realized, would be far too rigid and heartless to serve as the economic basis for a tolerable society. To be viable at all, such a system must provide at least some softening of the corners and relaxation of the rigid rule of self-interest.

Some of this relaxation comes, in the earlier stages of economic development, from the sheer lack of universality in the economic system itself. Not every economic good acquires at the outset the characteristics of inviolable private property; gleaners, squatters, and scavengers eke out an existence in the interstices of the formal system. But as property rights become all-encompassing and the system becomes more complex, the interstices change in character: they are no longer the refuge of the dispossessed but rather the arena for the nimble, the venturesome, and often the unscrupulous. Whether from a growing social conscience, an advancing ethical standard, or response to the sheer importunities of the indigent, some forms of succor for the unfortunate or the underprivileged emerge as a significant element in nearly all the more highly structured civilizations. These range from casual almsgiving through tax-supported public welfare systems to international aid such as that under the Marshall Plan.

Voluntarism Versus Compulsion

Given that there are important functions to be performed outside the economist's marketplace, it becomes appropriate to attempt to appraise the various institutions performing them. One scale on which they can be ranged is the degree to which the individual contribution is voluntary rather than compulsory. At the one extreme lies the alms given in secret, for which there is no motive beyond the desire to respond to the promptings of conscience, and at the other is the heavy hand of the tax collector, obtaining funds for purposes which in many cases overlap considerably with those for which strictly voluntary gifts are used. Ranging in between are contributions made under varying degrees of social or other pressure, such as the importunities of the panhandler, the sanctions of the clerical hierarchy, the threat of social ostracism, the withdrawal of such benefits as good will, or the superstitious fear of losing the favors of Dame Fortune. The history of the development of the welfare state can be told, in part, in terms of the growing need for works of public beneficence beyond the ability or at least the willingness of the public to respond voluntarily, and the substitution of tax-financed welfare disbursements for voluntary charity as a consequence. An ultrarationalist might claim that the result of this trend would be to so develop public welfare programs that there would be little or no need for private charity. While there has been a pronounced shift, in recent decades, in the relative roles of tax-supported and voluntary public welfare outlays, there are limits beyond which this trend does not seem likely to go. Under almost any conceivable development of the public sector, there will remain areas where voluntary support will be more appropriate; and in many areas, where either method of financing might be possible, voluntary financing has advantages that are not to be lost sight of.

Church and State

One of the largest areas in which voluntary giving is likely to remain the main resource is the support of religious institutions. To be sure, in a theocratic state, support of the church and support of the state are often so intermingled that the distinction between tax and tithe almost disappears. In countries with an established church, establishment usually carries with it some degree of financial support from funds collected in a compulsory manner, whether termed taxes or tithes; however, this can vary all the way from virtually complete support to a mere grant of minor special privileges.

Even where the principle of separation of church and state is the rule, various privileges accorded churches and similar institutions amount to a fairly substantial subsidy. In the United States, their property, amounting to some $15 billion, is largely exempt from property tax; at effective rates averaging probably between 1.5 and 2.5 per cent, this is an effective subsidy on the order of $300 million. Even greater is the subsidy in effect granted through the deduction allowed for contributions in computing the individual income tax: of $5.6 billion claimed for such contributions in 1958 returns itemizing deductions, probably $3 billion or more went to religious organizations.[1] This is deducted in returns with marginal rates averaging about 30 per cent, indicating a subsidy on the order of $900 million (in the sense that, had this $3 billion not been given to churches, $900 million of additional income tax would have been collected). In the face of subsidies thus aggregating over $1 billion a year to specifically religious activities, the furor over public aid to religiously controlled or sponsored education, to say nothing of the use of public school buses by parochial school students, brings up questions of the relative digestibility of gnats and camels.

Nevertheless, separation of church and state requires, at the very minimum, that religious institutions have sufficient voluntary support to eliminate the danger that subsidization, through tax exemption or otherwise, will provide an occasion for undue interference of the state in the affairs of the religious body, or vice versa. State subsidies in the form of deductions allowed for contributions have the virtue that they are distributed with reference to the independent voluntary support that the various institutions attract, so that the question of budgetary allocation does not arise. Conversely, since the allocation is automatic, there is little likelihood that lobbying for an increased share will arise, though we have seen that where the degree of interest in specific activities, such as church controlled schools, varies among faiths, a religious issue can become intermingled with political issues.

While preserving a nation from the taint of establishment on the

1 The American Association of Fund-Raising Counsel estimates that religion accounts for 51 per cent of all philanthropic giving, and presumably a larger proportion of individual than of corporate and foundation giving, but possibly a smaller proportion of upper income bracket giving covered by the standard deduction.

one hand and godless secularism on the other does require some voluntary support of religion, this support need not be completely private, as tax deductibility shows, nor need it be in all cases strictly gratuitous. Though most forms of "selling" religious services have their obnoxious features, it must be recorded that in the past considerable revenues have been obtained for religious organizations by practices that range from simony in its explicit form, through sale of indulgences, fees for marriages and other rites, to pew rentals, and the like. While many of these practices represent relatively innocuous ways of obtaining church funds, the lingering taint of simony on the one hand and commercialism on the other has led to their deemphasis. Even where fees are retained in conjunction with religious rites, either the amount is left largely to voluntary determination, or an amount is specified for the aesthetic elaboration of a ceremonial which, in more spartan form, is available without charge. While the practice is often inferior to the theory, the ideals usually expressed concerning the financing of religious institutions call for voluntary contributions commensurate with the means of the faithful, and sanctioned primarily by the urgings of the individual conscience, rather than by any threat of ostracism or of the withholding of ritual benefits.

The practical working out of the separation of church and state however, has led to many economically wasteful practices. In many instances, public educational facilities are unavailable for activities that have a religious or sectarian aspect. This is one factor in the complex of forces that has resulted in a quasi-duplication of educational facilities, one set being used five days a week for secular education and the other, generally inferior set, being used often only one-half day per week for religious education. The situation is at its extreme when, under "released time" arrangements, students are dismissed from public school ahead of the normal time in order that they be enabled to attend religious classes of a type approved by their parents, but in separate, and in some cases distant, facilities. There would seem to be a significant inconsistency in subsidizing the construction of religious facilities through tax exemption on the one hand, while on the other denying the use of alternative facilities that would otherwise be idle, on the grounds that this would involve the establishment of a religion by the state. To be sure, many religious groups would doubtless still wish to provide separate facilities that could be more closely integrated with the other activities of the congregation, but in terms of the economics involved, if they choose to do this it should only be after considering the full costs of the alternatives.

As is usually the case with special tax exemptions, those to religious bodies involve special problems and unintended effects. Restrictions on tax exemption of church property vary from one local jurisdiction to another. In rare cases exemption is applied to all property owned by a religious organization, regardless of character or use. Where the religious organization is in a position to derive explicit revenue from the property, an exemption so inclusive is obviously open to serious abuse: its benefits are capable of being multiplied beyond all reason through the expansion of activities only remotely related to any religious purpose. Not only is the loss of revenue a problem, but in many cases there is more or less direct competition with enterprise not favored with comparable tax privileges, and there are obvious grounds for complaint.

In order to prevent such abuses, exemption is more often limited to that part of the property devoted specifically to a religious use and not operated for revenue. But this also, when applied too rigorously, leads to economic waste. A common example is that of a church, located near a suburban shopping center and railroad station, which is encouraged, if not actually required by zoning ordinances, to provide a parking lot on its property for its congregation. This lot is then kept vacant during most of the week, though neighboring streets are parked as solid as the regulations will allow, lest the revenues that might be obtained from operating the parking space during the week be considered to forfeit the tax-exempt status of the property.

Even where appropriate adjustments are possible, so that the more obvious inefficiencies do not arise, there is a considerable bias introduced into the choice of means by which philanthropic purposes are served: land and buildings are favored with tax exemptions which do not apply to salaries.[2] To be sure, this may be regarded as merely the removal of a bias which otherwise afflicts economic activity in general, but even so, the consequences are probably inferior to what would result if a less prejudicial form of support for the activity were available.

2 Where education is concerned, this is another factor contributing indirectly to the tendency to provide bricks rather than brains.

Public and Private Contributions

Even outside the peculiarly sensitive area of religion, there are large areas where for one reason or another the more cumbersome apparatus of the state seems a less appropriate means of effecting the desired results than private contribution. In some cases this is because the activity in question appeals to a restricted class of individuals: the maintenance of a dog cemetery, or the maintenance of bird sanctuaries, or support for the climbing of Mt. Everest. Examples of this sort are, however, increasingly hard to find: Goddard's experiments with rockets could not find support through public appropriations, but we now find a million-fold expansion of his line of effort carried out with public funds. Private philanthropy very often provides limited means for initiating an activity which may later receive large public support once its value has been demonstrated.

In some cases the advantage of privately financed philanthropy arises from a greater freedom of action: the ability to discriminate in dispensing benefits, for example, may be necessary either to arrive at clear-cut results or to prevent the available resources from being spread uselessly thin; public auspices are more likely to find themselves handicapped either by beneficiaries who congest facilities, demanding a share as of right, or by sheer bureaucratic demands for some sort of uniformity. The Arrowsmith dilemma is often a vexing one, but when it occurs in a public operation the choice of long-run scientific advance rather than short-run palliative is much more likely to seem, to many, an abuse of power.

Another reason for entrusting an activity to privately financed agencies is the cumbersomeness of public agencies in dealing with relatively small-scale activities. To be sure, a considerable degree of improvement is possible in the administration of support for small projects through the establishment of subsidiary agencies, subcontracting, and the like, but there is always the basic conflict between, on the one hand, the expenditure of the time and effort of high-level decision-making bodies on matters of small magnitude in which they have relatively little basis for judgment, and on the other, the dilution of underlying accountability and responsibility to the point where there are excessive opportunities for waste or extravagance (or merely the undue promotion of the hobbies of individual administrators).

Closely related to this is the idea that activities financed through voluntary contributions are more efficiently and more economically carried out than when financed from public funds. Certainly administrators and employees of voluntary agencies who are aware that they are spending the widow's mite, or that the probability is slight that "there is more where that came from" are likely to be somewhat more concerned to use what they have carefully than where the vast resources of the state are available. An additional argument often cited is the fact that voluntary agencies are often able to secure conscientious work at wages that are considerably below the rates which comparable work would command in public employment, and below the going rates generally; in addition a considerable amount of free volunteer service is often obtainable. But too much should not be made of this: the response to the proposal for a Peace Corps indicates that under proper circumstances large amounts of volunteer effort can be mobilized under public as well as under private auspices; the ability to secure competent services at lower wage rates should properly be regarded not as an economy in the use of resources, but partly as the eliciting of an additional contribution in kind from these employees. It is possible that if these employees were to do the same work under public auspices at higher pay they would devote part of the difference to the support of other philanthropy. It is also possible that they derive more immediate satisfaction from doing the work under private auspices than they would under public; indeed, in a completely rational market this would be the necessary inference to be drawn from the fact of the wage differential.

To some extent, also, this efficiency differential may be considered a scale effect: where an activity is conducted on a large scale, and especially where it acquires a quasi-official status, as with the Red Cross, the identification of the administrator or employee with the contributor tends to diminish, and the pressure for efficiency tends to relax. Moreover, in large scale philanthropic enterprise there is often no clear-cut criterion of efficiency comparable to that provided in a large industrial organization whose accounting procedures provide allocated profits and losses as figures of merit. To this extent, then, the argument for voluntary activity on the basis of efficiency may be applicable primarily to activities that can be carried out on a small scale rather than those which by their nature require large scale effort.

Costs of Financing

Over-all efficiency is not merely a matter of expenditure of funds, but also of their collection. Here the picture is confused and the variety of situations is great. The marginal cost of public funds can be thought of as comprising three components: the marginal administrative cost of collecting increased sums in taxes, the marginal taxpayer compliance cost occasioned by an increase in the tax burden, and the marginal misallocation cost. Misallocation cost is the loss of economic efficiency which results from the distortions introduced into the operation of the economy by increasing tax rates and which induces more and more drastic adaptations, taken either directly or at several removes, to the changes in relative opportunities which the tax increase brings about. These adaptations may or may not have as a conscious intent the minimization of the tax burden. Rough ideas of average administration and compliance cost are comparatively easy to come by; the corresponding marginal costs may be somewhat more elusive, but in most cases will be relatively modest. Of course, one must be wary of estimating marginal administrative and compliance costs on the basis of the assumption that an increase in public expenditure is automatically to be covered by a simple increase in, say, the individual income tax rates. It cannot be concluded thereby that, since the only difference is in the size of the figures on the returns, these marginal costs will be negligible. Rate increases tend to provoke elaboration of the law, the litigation of issues that otherwise would not be raised, and increased evasion which in turn calls for increased countermeasures; moreover increased pressure for revenue may induce the introduction of new taxes. But by and large these costs will be minor. The misallocation cost is the great uncertainty, and in the absence of well-grounded estimates, opinions as to the magnitude of this cost will vary widely according to political complexion. A low over-all estimate for the cost of federal funds might run as low as 10 per cent, whereas for a hard pressed municipality with a poorly administered tax system the marginal cost of public funds might well run as high as 50 per cent.

The cost of voluntary contributions has a somewhat different composition. There is little here to correspond to the misallocation cost involved in taxation; it is difficult to think of potential contributors taking any drastic action to avoid the obligation to contribute, although some avoidance action may take place. Travellers may consciously or unconsciously avoid areas where beggars abound; in our own culture the prevalence of unlisted telephones may be, in small part, a corresponding phenomenon. But in the aggregate this is likely to be a negligible matter. Similarly, the time the individual takes in examining various appeals and discarding them or responding to them is probably far smaller in absolute amount than the effort expended in preparing tax returns, though in proportion to the total volume of contributions it may be more nearly comparable. The marginal effect may also be relatively larger: a larger aggregate of contributions probably means a larger number of appeals and of responses, to a much greater extent than a larger tax burden means a more numerous array of taxes.

The cost of solicitation is another matter. In cases bordering on fraud, costs have been known to cover a major fraction of the receipts. At best, even a minimal solicitation, acknowledgment, and maintenance of lists of contributors is likely to be a substantial fraction of the cost of operation. This is particularly true of any organization that depends on the repeated contributions of large numbers of small contributors rather than the special favor of a few large contributors or foundations.

The nominal costs of solicitation may not, however, be a true representation of social costs. A considerable amount is often spent for reports and other literature produced either as an essential part or as an adjunct to the principal activity of the agency. At one extreme the value of this information to the contributor as a matter of interest or usefulness may justify the cost of its distribution, wholly aside from any incidental effect that its distribution may have in encouraging contributions. At the other extreme the literature may be of little value except as a means of inducing the contributor to maintain his contributions. Since not much is available in the way of uniform reports on the outlays of philanthropic agencies, particularly of the smaller units, the question of where particular agencies draw the line between outlays for fund raising and outlays for other activities is largely academic.

Many agencies in raising funds find it psychologically effective to affix postage stamps to the return envelopes, which constitutes a somewhat different type of expense than that involved in other costs associated with fund raising. Since this involves a lower postage rate than when business reply envelopes are used, there may even be some saving in those cases where the response rate is high. To the extent that the rate differential reflects the extra cost to the post office of handling business reply mail, this saving is a genuine one in terms of resources. On the other hand if a fairly large percentage of the postage stamps remain unused, this is in effect a diversion of some of the contributed funds to the post office, as a kind of offset to the benefits of tax exemption. To the extent that some of the addressees are induced to spend time and effort salvaging the stamps, this is then of course part of the net social cost of the fund-raising operation. If this practice is psychologically effective, however, it probably impairs rather than improves the degree to which philanthropic contributions reflect the genuine underlying interests of the contributors.

There are other methods of raising philanthropic funds which have their own peculiarities, ranging from the church bazaar through bingo to the beaux-arts ball. The varied motivations for and benefits derived from these activities in addition to the fund-raising goal resist easy generalization. At one extreme the philanthropic aspect does little more than cast a mantle of respectability over indulgences that would otherwise be condemned; too often the price exacted for this cachet is absurdly low. In other instances the benefit becomes an activity worthwhile in its own right and needing only the catalyst of charitable purpose to bring it off. But there are many cases where a cold hard look at the relation between the results and the effort and sacrifice that went into them would produce a finding that the game was not worth the candle. To be sure, all ventures, whether for profit or for charity, entail some risk; the peculiar mixture of free and costly goods and services in philanthropy makes the evaluation of the results peculiarly difficult.

Interaction in Giving

There remains, however, perhaps the largest and the most difficult element in the social cost of voluntary and of public finance: the meaning to the contributor of giving up the amount contributed, voluntarily at one extreme and compulsorily at the other. A strict positivist might claim that in the case of a voluntary contribution the donor, on balance, gains in satisfaction at least as much as he would by spending the money in other ways (otherwise he would not have made the contribution). This might be valid in the case of an atomistically motivated contribution; in practice however we are in a situation akin to that of monopolistic competition where one's own behavior is expected to influence that of others, and so in making a choice one must allow not only for direct, but also for these indirect effects. The phrase sometimes used in connection with more substantial donations "in consideration of the gifts of others" is not a mere legal form but has economic substance. Financing a given public welfare service by taxation in a community of peers could then be considered merely a formalization of this implied agreement. Even if we set up a rigorous model of the situation, including the living standards of all members of the community as arguments in the utility function of each donor, it is no longer necessary to say that a donation by *A*, designed to increase the standard of living of *X*, *Y*, and *Z*, must yield *A* as much utility through this effect as it would if spent to raise *A*'s own standard of living. *A* will expect that *B* and *C* may also be induced by his gift to contribute to the same or similar objectives. The combined effects of *A*'s original gift plus that of the induced gifts on the standard of living of *X*, *Y*, and *Z* will provide for *A* a level of satisfaction equal to what he would have obtained had he kept the amount of his contribution for himself. Indeed, in some instances this interdependence of giving is formalized by the device of conditional or matching gifts, whereby a donor pledges to contribute a given amount provided that some specified amount is raised from other sources, or agrees to contribute in porportion to the gifts obtained from others. The donor might derive satisfaction from the direct consequences of his gift, sufficient to compensate him for making it, even without considering the effects of the gifts induced from others, but some fairly significant degree of interdependence does exist. From the point of view of welfare economics, this can be considered as a case of compounded external economies: not only do the expenditures of *X*, *Y*, and *Z* have favorable neighborhood effects on *A*, but the facilitating of these expenditures by *A* has favorable repercussions on *B* and *C*, and vice versa.

On the other side, it is not always clear that the payment of a tax or compulsory contribution is to be considered a clear net burden on the taxpayer, even before the benefits purchased with the tax are taken into consideration. If all similarly situated individuals are required to pay comparable tax increments, each taxpayer may feel relatively just as well off. In absolute terms, he may feel considerably better off than he would have felt if he had been singled out for a discriminatory levy. There is even some experimental evidence for this contention in the results of certain game experiments conducted at RAND and elsewhere. These indicate that at least in some situations in which the possibility of a competitive relationship is present there is a natural tendency on the part of individuals to maximize their relative rather than their absolute position. In the situations studied, two individuals not known to each other and having no direct means of communication with each other were asked to select on a given signal one of two actions, there being four possible combinations thus resulting. Previous to each series of trials each of the two individuals was shown a payoff matrix specifying the amounts that each player was to receive in the event of each of the four outcomes, the sum of the winnings of the two players being variable rather than constant. Results differed with variously structured payoff matrices, but the principle upon which a wider variety of the results could be rationalized than any other was that the players acted with the intention of maximizing the difference between their own winnings and those of their opponents.

There is, to be sure, a certain element of contradiction between a hypothesis that the motive of A is to outdo B and that hence B's success is a negative element in A's satisfaction, on the one hand, and that A can derive satisfaction from improvements in the situation of X, Y, and Z resulting from his gifts and those induced thereby from others. But this contradiction can probably be adequately resolved by assuming that where the individuals involved are of roughly comparable status, as A and B, the competitive or negative element may tend to predominate, particularly in a situation structured to resemble a game where success tends to be regarded as predominantly a relative matter, whereas between individuals such as A and X, comparability is so remote as to make any competitive element almost irrelevant, and the element of empathy becomes controlling.

This situation can be roughly pictured in the following diagram. We can think of individuals ranked along a line according to income or economic status, Y, relative to a particular individual A; the degree to which A obtains satisfaction from the welfare of others may be described in a curve $E_A(Y)$, which typically has a peak near A and tapers off in either direction, the exact shape depending on the temperament of the individual A; a secondary and fairly sharp peak may exist for some charismatic leadership group near the top of the status scale. Similarly, we can describe the influence of the typical rivalry between A and others in a curve $R_A(Y)$, somewhat similar to $E_A(Y)$, but much more sharply peaked, dropping off rapidly to a level of practically zero within a relatively short distance on either side. Rivalry being a negative interaction and empathy a positive one, by subtracting R from E we get the net interaction or neighborhood effect, $N_A(Y)$, which may be negative in the neighborhood of A, but can be thought of as having a positive peak at an income some distance below Y_A, and possibly one or two other peaks at an income above Y_A. Further, we can draw a marginal utility of income curve $U_A(Y)$, as perceived by A, representing the amount of satisfaction that A thinks individuals at different income levels will receive from an increment of income (or of expenditure on their behalf) and multiply

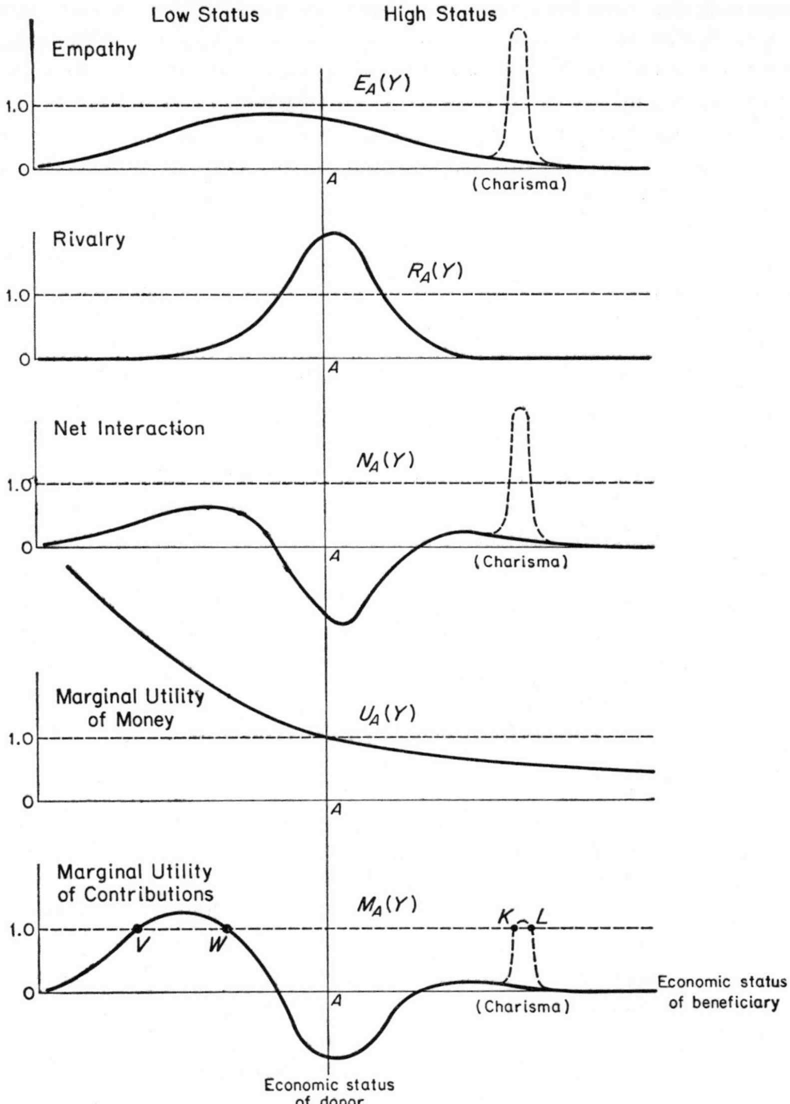

$N_A(Y)$ by $U_A(Y)$, and also by a factor representing the "contagion effect" of *A*'s contributions on the contributions of others (it would be very difficult to say anything specific about the variation of this contagion effect between contributions for activities benefiting different income levels); the result can be shown as a curve $M_A(Y)$, representing the marginal utility to A of a contribution by him for the benefit of persons of status Y. If a horizontal line is drawn at a level representing the marginal utility of income to A, cutting $M_A(Y)$ at V and W, and possibly also at K and L, then the individuals in the status range indicated by V and W can be considered the natural objects of A's bounty. The possible KL range can be considered to cover the case of the charwoman who knits a shawl for the princess, or more generally of the MP who as her representative votes for a substantial civil list, though cases of this sort can be fitted only somewhat awkwardly into such a scheme.

Of course, in addition to distances measured by income or economic status, there will also be distances in terms of age, race, culture, geographic location, and other characteristics to which a similar discussion might apply.

The net result of these considerations seems to be that it is not possible to say anything very definite from a strictly behavioral point of view on the relative subjective sacrifice involved in the making of a gift and the payment of a tax, though on balance the evidence may seem to point to the tax as more painful than the gift, but not by anything like the amount of loss suffered, say, if the same quantum of resources had been destroyed by some uninsured catastrophe.

Philanthropy and Redistribution

Private and public philanthropy are both often regarded primarily as instruments for the redistribution of resources so as to diminish economic inequalities. But the differences between the degree to which public and private philanthropy accomplish this are probably much more striking, in terms of the evidence available, than casual observation would lead one to expect. The analysis of the preceding section might indicate that the natural objects of philanthropy of a given economic stratum are those located only a moderate distance down the scale, rather than at the bottom. Such data as we have as to the character of giving indicate that the difference in economic level between donor and beneficiary is comparatively small. According to the 1950 BLS–Wharton School sample survey, 32.6 per cent of all gifts were in the nature of family and reciprocity gifts having a minimal redistributional content; 21.4 per cent were gifts for the support of individuals, including alimony, representing some redistribution, but in most cases largely among relatives and spanning a relatively narrow spread of status. Another 29.4 per cent of all giving was to religious institutions, and while these might be thought of as agencies through which redistribution would take place, a very large fraction of this amount is spent for the maintenance of activities in the congregation, and only a minor fraction finds its way to the support of outside activities. Moreover, as public welfare agencies have taken over a large portion of the burden of caring for the indigent, the channeling of alms through religious agencies has correspondingly diminished in importance. Further, the ratio of gifts to religious organizations to discretionary receipts was remarkably constant over all the income levels covered by this survey. To consider that redistribution amounts to any very substantial part of this category of contribution would require the assumption that the individual's share in the consumption of religious services constitutes, in technical economic terms, a very "inferior" good, indeed!

The next largest single category among objects of individual philanthropy is education. Here again, casual observation suggests that the beneficiaries tend to belong to social and economic strata not very far removed from those of the donors: private schools and colleges are supported in considerable measure by their own graduates; students at such institutions are often drawn from social strata not far removed from those of the chief benefactors, and even scholarship holders come in large measure from middle class rather than the poorest strata in the population. Indeed, some of the giving of this kind could well be regarded as the repayment of a loan or at least of the reciprocation of a previous gift, and thus have no redistributive consequences at all.

Not enough is known about the remainder of private philanthropy to warrant much being said without further appraisal. But the overall picture would appear to remain one in which the role of philanthropy in redistribution is relatively slight.

This impression is somewhat reinforced by the examination of the figures available from income tax returns on the distribution of charitable contributions by income classes. Data on contributions are unfortunately limited to those returns of taxpayers who elect to itemize deductions; in 1958, the latest year for which data are available, such returns were only 35 per cent of the total number, though they accounted for slightly over half of the adjusted gross income. As shown in Table 1, the proportion of returns that itemize deductions increases steadily with income. It can be presumed therefore that, since a relatively large amount of contributions would be one of the factors inducing taxpayers to itemize, *ceteris paribus,* the itemizing taxpayers

TABLE

REGRESSIVITY OF NET CHARITABLE
(money figures in

Adjusted Gross Income Class	Total No. of Returns (1)	No. of Itemizing Returns (2)	Percentage of Returns Itemizing (3)	Gross Contributions of Itemizers (4)
None	384,258	—	—	—
Under .6	3,950,030	26,090	0.66	2,164
.6 to 1.0	3,060,247	207,591	6.78	14,435
1.0 to 1.5	4,120,276	451,900	10.97	41,067
1.5 to 2	3,570,536	613,555	17.18	66,235
2 to 2.5	3,689,218	845,169	22.91	104,089
2.5 to 3	3,723,909	962,390	25.84	134,649
3 to 3.5	3,742,848	1,126,380	30.09	176,263
3.5 to 4	3,729,578	1,304,349	34.97	218,021
4 to 4.5	3,745,242	1,452,898	38.79	263,750
4.5 to 5	3,639,977	1,574,279	43.25	298,951
5 to 6	6,375,555	3,253,856	51.04	654,731
6 to 7	4,676,947	2,605,487	55.71	602,241
7 to 8	3,226,844	1,797,271	55.70	457,855
8 to 9	2,171,701	1,223,286	56.33	348,207
9 to 10	1,452,594	795,245	54.75	252,924
10 to 15	2,488,095	1,496,835	60.16	610,286
15 to 20	588,262	425,450	72.32	249,564
20 to 25	264,732	213,829	80.77	161,334
25 to 50	369,939	325,166	87.90	373,703
50 to 100	91,715	88,070	96.03	254,865
100 to 150	14,080	13,811	98.09	99,799
150 to 200	3,863	3,804	98.47	48,984
200 to 500	3,956	3,934	99.44	115,374
500 to 1,000	536	534	99.63	47,424
1,000 & over	244	243	99.59	96,921
Total	59,085,182	20,811,422	35.22	5,693,836

1

CONTRIBUTIONS, 1958
thousands of dollars)

Adjusted Gross Income of Itemizers (5)	Col. 4 / Col. 5 (per cent) (6)	Net Cost of Contrib-tions (7)	Disposable Income (8)	Col. 7 / Col. 8 (per cent) (9)
—	—	—	—	—
10,046	21.54	2,164	a	a
174,300	8.28	13,626	116,505	11.70
578,099	7.10	37,343	386,684	9.66
1,077,804	6.15	58,034	757,164	7.66
1,905,776	5.46	89,656	1,392,209	6.44
2,653,578	5.07	114,048	1,970,476	5.79
3,659,665	4.82	146,627	2,731,357	5.37
4,900,598	4.45	179,374	3,681,170	4.87
6,172,608	4.27	214,427	4,634,058	4.63
7,481,243	4.00	249,627	5,639,531	4.43
17,837,342	3.67	539,887	13,343,556	4.05
16,861,809	3.57	485,414	12,580,871	3.86
13,430,839	3.41	366,550	9,959,190	3.68
1,354,116	3.36	271,653	7,645,980	3.55
7,525,975	3.36	197,250	5,527,028	3.57
17,710,772	3.45	473,574	13,005,654	3.64
7,297,241	3.42	172,665	5,323,023	3.24
4,758,024	3.39	104,426	3,418,940	3.05
10,913,850	3.42	207,649	7,460,084	2.78
5,823,403	4.38	93,790	3,553,809	2.64
1,615,248	6.18	26,244	923,337	2.84
651,423	7.52	9,970	377,432	2.64
1,109,114	10.40	12,440	649,997	1.91
357,883	13.25	4,172	231,307	1.80
498,205	19.45	8,481	353,896	2.40
145,358,961	3.92	4,079,091	105,663,258	3.86

[a] Negative disposable income.

will, on the average within each income class, make relatively greater contributions than nonitemizing taxpayers. Nevertheless, over ranges where the proportion of itemizing taxpayers does not change too abruptly, the figures presented in Table 1 represent reasonably well the degree to which contributions are concentrated in the upper income classes.

Column 6 shows the crude ratio of gross contributions reported to the adjusted gross income of itemizers. It is seen that in the lower income classes singling out the itemizers is highly selective of those taxpayers with relatively large contributions. This selectiveness is somewhat less severe as incomes increase; the proportion of contributions drops to a low of 3.36 per cent in the $8,000–$9,000 class, thereafter rising gradually to a maximum of nearly 20 per cent for incomes over one million dollars. This is a reasonably progressive showing, particularly as the maximum limit for the individual on the deduction of contributions is in most cases 30 per cent of adjusted gross income.

To assess properly the effect of contributions on the distribution of income, however, it is necessary to consider the fact that only part of the gross contribution reported represents a net sacrifice to the taxpayer; depending on the marginal tax rate, a fairly substantial part of the cost of the contributions represents a reduction in the tax that would otherwise have become due. On the basis of a composite weighted mean marginal rate, derived from the marginal rates for the various categories of taxpayers in each income class, the net cost of the contributions is given in column 7. It is appropriate to consider this net cost in relation to the net disposable income the taxpayer would have had, had he made no contributions (see col. 8 of Table 1). This is obtained by taking total income, correcting it to reflect in full the capital gains and losses reported for the current year, subtracting all allowable deductions, and also the income tax itself, and adding the cost of the contributions as given in column 7. The resulting ratios are given in column 9, where it is apparent that instead of the proportion of contributions increasing with income, there is a substantial and steady decrease in the percentage of disposable income sacrificed, except for a modest increase in the top income class.

These figures are also, of course, subject to considerable bias through the selective effect of considering only itemizing returns, but this factor is hardly sufficient to change the general picture for income classes above $5,000. There are other biases that would tend to strengthen the trend shown: in the absence of data, no adjustment was made to include tax exempt interest and similar items in the disposable income. Nor are capital gains unreported for income tax purposes represented in the figures, whether because the assets are held to the death of the taxpayer or, more relevantly for present purposes, because they are used as the medium in which the gift is made. In this latter increasingly frequent case, not only is the gain not reported, but the full market value of the asset is used as the basis for the charitable deduction, so that the cost of the contribution is even less, on this account, than that shown in the table. While this practice is one well-known to fund raisers, there are no data available on its magnitude. Its prevalence, however, should quiet any qualms that one might have about the inclusion of realized capital gains in a disposable income figure to which the cost of the contribution is to be related.

To what extent does the tax deductibility of gifts stimulate giving? Unfortunately the data available provide very little evidence on this question. At the lower level, we do have separate data for taxable and nontaxable returns at the various income levels, but the effect of selecting only itemized returns is to make the ratio of gifts to disposable income uniformly higher for the nontaxable returns (Table 2). Also, since the classification of returns is by adjusted gross income, returns in a given income class are more likely to be nontaxable if they have large contributions. The combined effect of these two influences is to mask completely any possible tendency for the tax deduc-

TABLE 2

CONTRIBUTIONS IN TAXABLE AND NONTAXABLE RETURNS, WITH ITEMIZED DEDUCTIONS, 1958

ADJUSTED GROSS INCOME CLASS (thousands of dollars)	TAXABLE RETURNS			NONTAXABLE RETURNS			*Ratios of Gross Contribution to Adjusted Gross Income* (per cent)		*Ratios of Net Cost of Contribution to Disposable Income* (per cent)	
		Itemizing			*Itemizing*					
	Total Number	Number	Per Cent of Total	Total Number	Number	Per Cent of Total	Tax.	Nontax.	Tax.	Nontax.
None	—	—	—	384,258	—	—	—	[a]	—	[b]
Under .6	—	—	—	3,950,030	26,090	0.66	—	21.54	—	[b]
.6 to 1.0	1,296,407	67,066	5.17	1,763,840	140,525	7.97	6.76	9.07	6.51	15.56
1.0 to 1.5	2,127,075	228,159	10.73	1,993,201	223,741	11.23	6.42	7.79	6.91	13.12
1.5 to 2.0	2,111,329	389,618	18.45	1,459,207	223,937	15.34	5.94	6.51	6.31	10.63
2.0 to 2.5	2,537,591	584,426	23.03	1,151,627	260,743	22.64	5.45	5.49	5.82	7.96
2.5 to 3.0	2,807,388	744,640	26.52	916,521	217,750	23.76	5.02	5.26	5.34	7.38
3.0 to 3.5	3,062,908	948,514	30.97	679,940	177,866	26.15	4.80	4.88	5.09	7.00
3.5 to 4.0	3,232,549	1,147,777	35.51	497,029	156,572	31.50	4.37	5.06	4.59	7.09
4.0 to 4.5	3,488,552	1,339,914	38.41	256,690	112,984	44.01	4.22	4.91	4.45	6.82
4.5 to 5.0	3,465,499	1,488,801	42.96	174,478	85,478	48.99	3.97	4.45	4.32	6.39
5.0 and over	21,522,836	12,114,799	56.29	206,227	132,022	64.17	3.66	7.04	3.47	12.17
Total	45,652,134	19,053,714	41.74	13,433,048	1,757,708	13.08	3.85	5.80	3.71	8.73

[a] Negative adjusted gross income.
[b] Negative disposable income

TABLE 3

EFFECTS OF TAXABILITY AND NONITEMIZING ON REPORTED CONTRIBUTIONS, 1940–41

INCOME CLASSES [a] (thousands of dollars)		THOUSANDS OF RETURNS Itemizing 1940	Itemizing 1941	Nonitemizing 1940	Nonitemizing 1941	Percentage of Returns Itemizing 1940	Percentage of Returns Itemizing 1941	Ratio of Gross Contributions to Net Income in Itemizing Returns (per cent) 1940	1941
0 to 1	Taxable	529	794	—	894	100	47.0	2.86	4.24
	Nontaxable	1383	1143	—	369	100	75.6	2.67	3.58
	Total	1912	1937	—	1263	100	60.5	2.73	3.90
1 to 2	Taxable	2905	3403	—	3277	100	50.9	2.68	3.21
	Nontaxable	2108	2334	—	2527	100	48.0	1.56	1.93
	Total	5013	5737	—	5804	100	49.7	2.19	2.70
2 to 2.5	Taxable	914	2317	—	1275	100	64.5	2.12	2.41
	Nontaxable	2545	553	—	958	100	36.6	0.92	1.58
	Total	3459	2870	—	2233	100	56.2	1.25	2.25
2.5 to 3	Taxable	912	1695	—	753	100	69.2	2.10	2.33
	Nontaxable	887	150	—	199	100	43.0	1.03	1.54
	Total	1799	1845	—	952	100	66.0	1.56	2.27
3 to 4	Taxable	1014	1644	—	—	100	100	2.08	2.04
	Nontaxable	6	33	—	—	100	100	1.23	1.14
	Total	1020	1677	—	—	100	100	1.93	2.02
4 to 5	Taxable	394	514	—	—	100	100	2.11	2.12
	Nontaxable	[b]	1	—	—	100	100	(1.80)	(1.27)
	Total	394	515	—	—	100	100	2.11	2.12

[a] Itemizing returns by net income; nonitemizing, by gross income.
[b] Less than 500.

tion in taxable returns to induce a higher level of giving. Data for earlier years is available by net income classes, and without the complication of the nonitemizing return; the data for 1940 and 1941 are compared in Table 3, showing the effect of the introduction of the standard deduction for returns under $3,000; Table 4 compares 1943 and 1944, showing the effect of extending the standard deduction privilege to incomes above $3,000. However, the data are open to the interpretation that the taxability of the return merely makes the taxpayer more careful to list all of his contributions, whereas the filer of the nontaxable return may simply not bother to list all of his deductions, even though his contributions may be just as large.

TABLE 4

EFFECTS OF TAXABILITY AND NONITEMIZING ON REPORTED CONTRIBUTIONS, 1943–44

INCOME CLASSES[a] (thousands of dollars)		THOUSANDS OF RETURNS Itemizing 1943	*Itemizing* 1944	*Nonitemizing* 1943	*Nonitemizing* 1944	*Per Cent of Returns Itemizing* 1943	1944	*Ratio of Gross Contributions to Net Income in Itemizing Returns* (per cent) 1943	1944
Taxable and Nontaxable Returns									
Negative	Nontaxable	17	192	—	—	100.0	100.0	—	b
0 to 0.5	Taxable	218	—	—	—	100.0	—	8.33	—
	Nontaxable	644	80	1601	3181	28.7	2.4	4.62	9.70
	Total	862	80	1601	3181	35.0	2.4	5.55	9.70
0.5 to 0.75	Taxable	754	131	1293	1914	36.8	6.4	5.06	5.80
	Nontaxable	208	159	376	693	35.6	18.7	2.03	9.43
	Total	962	290	1669	1607	36.6	15.3	4.45	7.46
0.75 to 1.00	Taxable	1106	304	2016	2646	35.4	9.6	4.46	6.57
	Nontaxable	121	103	95	117	56.0	46.8	2.38	6.76
	Total	1227	407	2111	2763	36.7	12.8	4.25	6.61
1.00 to 1.25	Taxable	1332	412	2276	3065	36.9	11.9	4.25	6.54
	Nontaxable	128	66	111	71	53.5	48.2	1.50	8.28
	Total	1460	478	2387	3136	38.0	13.2	4.01	6.72
1.25 to 1.50	Taxable	1467	469	2313	3044	38.8	13.4	3.89	6.30
	Nontaxable	—	95	—	—	—	100.0	—	7.39
	Total	1467	564	2313	3044	38.8	15.6	3.89	6.45
Taxable									
1.50 to 1.75		1517	512	2371	2947	39.0	14.8	3.64	6.15
1.75 to 2.00		1646	523	2135	2880	43.5	15.4	3.38	5.70
2.00 to 2.25		1628	513	1842	2617	46.9	16.4	3.20	5.50
2.25 to 2.50		1579	511	1556	2359	50.4	17.8	1.86	5.33
2.50 to 2.75		1446	519	1289	2268	52.9	18.6	3.09	5.02
2.75 to 3.00		1680	495	1069	2019	61.1	19.7	2.74	4.89
3.0 to 3.5		2991	873	—	3260	100.0	21.1	2.42	4.83
3.5 to 4.0		1685	621	—	2165	100.0	22.3	2.37	4.72
4.0 to 4.5		902	422	—	1356	100.0	23.7	2.32	4.77
4.5 to 5.0		509	273	—	766	100.0	26.3	2.27	4.46
5 to 6		469	305	—	628	100.0	32.7	2.27	4.49
6 to 7		250	174	—	244	100.0	41.6	2.31	4.38
7 to 8		166	97	—	123	100.0	44.1	2.26	4.04
8 to 9		120	73	—	78	100.0	48.3	2.28	3.93
9 to 10		95	58	—	54	100.0	51.8	2.25	3.85
10 to 15		231	180	—	118	100.0	60.4	2.11	3.52
15 to 20		101	93	—	14	100.0	71.5	2.12	3.21
20 to 25		54	53	—	14	100.0	79.1	2.15	3.07

[a] For 1943, net income; for 1944, adjusted gross income.
[b] Negative income.

TABLE 5

PROGRESSIVITY OF NET CHARITABLE BEQUESTS, 1959
(money figures in thousands of dollars)

GROSS ESTATE CLASSES	TAXABLE AND NONTAXABLE ESTATES			NONTAXABLE ESTATES		
		Net Cost of Charitable Bequests			*Net Cost of Charitable Bequests*	
	Disposable Estate (1)	Amount (2)	Per Cent of Disposable Estate (3)	Disposable Estate (4)	Amount (5)	Per Cent of Disposable Estate (6)
0 to 60	450	—	—	450	—	—
60 to 70	365,685	7,138	1.95	250,625	7,033	2.81
70 to 80	426,829	7,671	1.80	192,765	7,069	3.67
80 to 90	403,697	9,303	2.30	183,464	8,353	4.55
60 to 100	386,049	6,534	1.69	180,359	5,560	3.08
100 to 120	694,739	12,846	1.85	315,741	10,399	3.29
120 to 150	825,212	17,218	2.09	153,383	12,914	8.42
150 to 200	928,677	22,930	2.47	44,413	16,805	37.84
200 to 300	1,101,702	30,580	2.78	29,005	17,784	61.31
300 to 500	1,062,246	41,110	3.87	22,598	19,233	85.11
500 to 1,000	1,111,714	57,663	5.19	19,051	16,212	83.13
1,000 to 2,000	714,490	44,834	6.27	8,737	7,544	86.35
2,000 to 3,000	280,095	35,316	12.61	5,191	3,748	72.20
3,000 to 5,000	224,218	28,731	12.65	2,421	2,382	98.39
5,000 to 10,000	205,581	22,705	11.04	4,607	1,707	37.05
10,000 to 20,000	131,592	12,466	9.47	—	—	—
20,000 and up	68,793	23,283	33.85	—	—	—
Total [a]	9,068,299	516,447	5.695	1,435,603	159,536	11.11

[a] Calculated from average ratios.

Other somewhat inconclusive evidence may be gleaned from estate tax returns. Here the calculation of the ratio of net cost of contribution to net disposable estate shows a definite though somewhat irregular increase with size of gross estate (Tables 5 and 6). On the whole one would expect that a wealthy taxpayer, anxious to take full advantage of the tax deduction, would do his giving during his lifetime so as to obtain the benefit of the income tax deduction in addition to the avoidance of the estate tax. But of course a similar argument could be made in favor of noncharitable *inter vivos* dispositions to take advantage of the gift tax. In some cases earlier disposition during

TABLE 6

EFFECTS OF CLASSIFICATION BASIS ON CHARITABLE BEQUEST RATIOS, 1959

CLASSIFICATION BY NET ESTATE [a]			CLASSIFICATION BY GROSS ESTATE			
Net Estate Classes (thousands of dollars) (1)	*Charitable Bequests as Percentage of Gross Estate* (2)	*Average Gross Estate* (thousands of dollars) (3)	*Gross Estate Classes* (thousands of dollars) (4)	*Charitable Bequests as Percentage of Gross Estate* All Estates (5)	Taxable Estates (6)	Nontaxable Estates (7)
Jnder 60	—	52.0	Under 60	—	—	—
			60 to 70	1.78	0.09	2.51
			70 to 80	1.64	0.26	3.25
			80 to 90	2.11	0.44	4.08
			90 to 100	1.55	0.49	2.77
0 to 80	1.97	102.5	100 to 120	1.70	0.69	2.96
0 to 100	3.65	132.3	120 to 150	1.92	0.71	6.90
00 to 150	2.82	173.5	150 to 200	2.34	0.80	26.49
50 to 200	3.76	248.9	200 to 300	2.86	1.38	46.91
00 to 300	3.28	340.3	300 to 500	3.91	2.31	66.19
00 to 400	3.54	486.1				
00 to 500	5.22	633.4				
00 to 600	11.40	801.7	500 to 1,000	5.44	4.06	73.13
00 to 700	4.81	907.8				
00 to 800	11.54	1,105.4				
00 to 900	4.59	1,147.5	1,000 to 2,000	6.77	5.82	72.55
00 to 1,000	3.97	1,250.5				
,000 to 2,000	7.26	1,818.1				
			2,000 to 3,000	14.07	12.97	76.82
,000 to 3,000	13.76	3,425.5	3,000 to 5,000	15.16	14.17	92.12
,000 to 4,000	5.70	5,129.0				
,000 to 5,000	28.07	8,350.0	5,000 to 10,000	15.36	14.84	48.68
,000 to 7,000	8.05	7,799.0				
,000 to 10,000	7.08	11,847.0	10,000 to 20,000	17.20	17.20	—
0,000 to 20,000	4.06	19,246.0				
0,000 and over	0.16	31,676.0	20,000 and over	52.03	52.03	—
Total	5.10	259.5	Total	5.74	5.10	9.66

[a] Taxable estates only.

the lifetime of the donor may run up against the 30 per cent limit on the deductibility of charitable contributions in the income tax, whereas no corresponding limit exists for the estate tax. On the whole, the evidence would seem to indicate that, viewed as demand for a commodity whose price is reduced by the tax deductibility, demand for "gross charity" has an elasticity smaller than one, and that, while the deductibility may increase the gross amount of contributions, it does so by less than the tax relief granted. The net effect, therefore, is to decrease the aggregate amount of net sacrifice incurred by the donors, the increase in the proceeds to the beneficiaries being a burden borne entirely by the fisc. One may well question whether it is sound public policy to thus subsidize much more heavily the charities favored by the wealthy as distinct from those appealing primarily to the poorer contributors.

Although I have not looked into this matter recently, my impression from earlier surveys is that the United States is almost unique in the degree to which charitable contributions are subsidized through tax exemption. In the United Kingdom, in order to qualify for exemption, the gift must take the form of a transfer of income, in line with the British predilection for considering only more or less repetitive transfers as entitled to consideration under the income tax. In effect, a donor must enter into a covenant with the beneficiary to pay a stated sum regularly for a period of five years or more; when he makes these payments he withholds the normal income tax, and the beneficiary as an exempt entity is entitled to put in a claim for a refund of the tax thus withheld on its income. It is not clear to what extent, if any, this has the psychological effect of inducing the donor to make a net payment of as much as the gross gift would have been without the tax, so making the tax refund a net increment to the resources of the beneficiary, or whether only the same gross gift tends to be made in any case.

The most clear-cut cases of tax-induced philanthropy seem to derive from the estate tax, where the establishment of a philanthropic foundation under friendly control may be the means of avoiding the dissolution or loss of control of a family corporate empire. It has been claimed that this was a significant factor in the creation of the Ford Foundation. While these instances are striking when they occur, they are probably relatively few in number.

If there were a substantial response of philanthropic contributions to the inducement of income tax deductibility it would seem that it would show up in a comparison of data for 1930–31, when the top

TABLE 7

EFFECTS OF RATE INCREASES ON CONTRIBUTION RATIOS, 1930–33

Net Income Classes (thousands of dollars)	*Marginal Tax Rate, Per Cent*		*Gross Contributions as a Percentage of Net Income*				*Net Cost of Contributions as a Percentage of Disposable Income*			
	1930–31	1932–33	1930	1931	1932	1933	1930	1931	1932	1933
00 to 150	25	56	3.68	4.41	4.87	3.60	3.01	3.86	6.02	2.81
50 to 200	25	37	3.86	4.26	5.75	3.73	3.25	4.02	6.08	3.77
00 to 250	25	58	3.89	4.87	6.04	3.92	3.28	4.56	16.34	3.24
50 to 300	25	58	4.01	4.45	4.72	3.96	3.35	4.04	5.87	2.88
00 to 400	25	59	4.29	5.03	7.37	3.44	3.53	4.55	5.89	4.08
00 to 500	25	60	4.48	5.10	6.40	3.98	3.74	4.28	6.62	3.13
00 to 750	25	61	4.39	5.79	7.00	3.97	3.61	4.95	[a]	2.65
50 to 1000	25	62	4.90	6.28	5.37	5.62	3.98	6.60	4.45	2.90
Over 1000	25	63	6.86	6.24	8.67	3.58	5.62	5.72	9.53	2.34
Over 500	25	62±	6.01	6.14	7.29	3.99	4.92	5.63	12.50	2.52
Over 100	25	59±	4.67	5.11	6.04	3.80	4.13	4.62	9.07	2.93
All returns			2.72	2.92	3.30	2.68				

[a] Negative disposable income due to large capital losses.

combined normal and surtax rates were 25 per cent on incomes over $100,000, and 1932–33 when the rates at these income levels were more than doubled, to from 56 per cent to 63 per cent. But examination of this material, as presented in Table 7, indicates no such responsiveness.

External Economies and Diseconomies in Fund Raising

The pursuit of the contributor's dollar has obvious external economies and diseconomies not greatly dissimilar to those encountered in any kind of selling activity. There is, on the one hand, the likelihood that funds obtained through appeal may impinge on the funds available for other contributions, and on the other, that appeals may reinforce each other by enhancing the general level of giving. It is hard to determine just what would be the socially optimal proportion of effort to put into fund-raising activities. Aside from curbing the more extreme practices that take undue advantage of psychological predilections or that verge on fraud, it is not clear just what modifying influences would, on balance, be in the public interest.

Contributions and Macro-Economic Equilibrium

There is a sense in which the claim of the advertising industry that it is a great creator of aggregate demand has a counterpart in the soliciting of charitable contributions: to the extent that they are made out of savings and that the proceeds are immediately disbursed, the contributions tend to be a stimulus to the economy. Of course this stimulus will be desirable or undesirable according to whether the economy is or is not suffering from underemployment. If contributions were relatively higher in periods of depression than in prosperity, as seems to some slight extent to be the case, they would constitute a stabilizing factor in the economy. It may be doubted, however, whether this is more true of charitable contributions than of many forms of personal expenditure.

On the other hand, to the extent that charitable gifts or bequests are made in the form of endowment funds, there may be a depressing effect on the economy; the gift may have the effect of reducing the level of expenditure of the donor or of those who would have been his beneficiaries in the absence of the charitable bequest. Probably this effect is not large enough to be a primary concern.

Summary

The main suggestion that emerges from the above discussion is that the methods and degree of public support to privately controlled philanthropy needs to be thoroughly reexamined. Complete absence of any subsidy of religion by the state is a gross fiction. Tax exemption, particularly the deduction under the income tax, seems to be much more an expression of the general predilection in this country for privately organized and controlled philanthropy rather than a significant stimulus to *net* giving. A concession that seemed moderate enough when originally introduced has grown and changed shape with increases in tax rates and the complexities of the law, so as to produce results that are not only bizarre on occasion, but in their over-all pattern seem to conform to no defensible social policy. The unacknowledged and haphazard array of subsidies that result from present special tax privileges call for replacement with more uniform and explicit arrangements that can be brought into line with desirable public policy.

Notes on a Theory of Philanthropy

KENNETH E. BOULDING
University of Michigan

IN VIEW of the importance of philanthropy in our society, it is surprising that so little attention has been given to it by economic or social theorists. In economic theory, especially, the subject is almost completely ignored. This is not, I think, because economists regard mankind as basically selfish or even because economic man is supposed to act only in his self-interest; it is rather because economics has essentially grown up around the phenomenon of exchange and its theoretical structure rests heavily on this process. Exchange is a reciprocal transfer. Philanthropy, apparently, represents a unilateral transfer. In an exchange, something is transferred from party *A* to party *B* and something else from *B* to *A*. The ratio of these two quantities is, of course, the ratio of exchange and if one of the exchangeables is money, then this ratio is a price. The price system is a basic one for the economist and he tends to regard society as being organized by it. This is true even in national income economics for money income always represents quantity of commodity multiplied by its price. In a single transfer or gift, however, there is no price, for nothing is given in exchange. The economist, hence, feels rather at sea. When he finds himself in an area of social life which is apparently priceless, he hardly knows what to do.

It is tempting for the economist to argue that there are really no gifts and that all transactions involve some kind of exchange, that is, some kind of *quid pro quo*. If we drop a dime in the blind man's cup, it is because the blind man gives us something. We feel a certain glow of emotional virtue, and it is this that we receive for our dime. Looked at from the point of view of the recipient, we might suppose that the blind man gives out a commodity or service which consists in being pitiable. Even if we look upon the transaction as an exchange, however, it is clearly a very curious one. The dime in the cup is a clear enough transfer of assets from the donor to the recipient. What passes from the recipient to the donor, however, is mysterious. There is no conservation of assets here. The glow of self-righteousness which is felt by the donor may have no corresponding emotion, feeling, or disutility in the mind of the blind man. That which is in some sense cost to the blind man, that is, what he gives up, is not the same thing as the receipt to the donor. This phenomenon, of course, is not peculiar to the situation of the pure gift. It is true of almost any transaction or exchange involving services. Thus, we are familiar with the fact that in the wage bargain, what the worker gives up is not what the employer receives. Even though what the employer gives up is physically what the worker receives (money), the significance of the cost to the employer may be very different from that of the receipt to the worker. We have here a transaction which is much more complicated than the simple exchange of wheat for money on the wheat market, in which what is given up by the seller is of the same order as what is received by the buyer. It begins to look, therefore, as if some of the peculiarities of philanthropy penetrate rather deeply into the economic system.

We should notice, also, that the basic concept of the gift, that is, the unilateral or one-way transfer, extends far beyond what is usually thought of as philanthropy. It applies to anything which may be classified as a transfer payment, whether this is made by the private donor, a foundation, or by government. Transfer payments, especially the payments by government, are coming to be an increasing element in our economic life. They presumably have much the same kind of impact on the economy that philanthropic gifts have, although their legal position and their mode of organization may be very different.

It might be argued, therefore, that all unilateral transfers whether these are the transfer payments of government, for instance, in agricultural subsidies or social security payments, or whether they are the grants of foundations, or even simple gifts among individuals, should be regarded as elements in what Talcott Parsons calls the "polity" rather than the economy. A very interesting question, somewhat peripheral to the main issue, is whether interest payments or even bank loans should be regarded as part of the system of unilateral transfers; that is, again, as elements in the polity. There is here, it is true, a form of exchange over time—an exchange of money now for money later. In the immediate present, however, this looks very much like the unilateral transfer and the curious attitude of the United States government towards interest payments, which it allows as a deduction from income in much the same way as charitable contributions, is an indication and recognition of the peculiar status of this form of transfer. What we have here is clearly a continuum with ordinary acts of exchange at one end and charitable gifts at the other, but with a great many intermediate forms and stages.

Just as a loan may be regarded as a short-run gift but as a long-run exchange, so may outright gifts be in this category. In some societies, indeed, almost all gifts are essentially what the anthropologists call "silent trade"; that is, almost always made in the expectation of a return gift. It has been argued by some anthropologists that gifts essentially antedate exchange as a social institution, and that exchange arises out of a mutual transfer of gifts. In our society the exchange of gifts at Christmas is perhaps a case in point. Even though it is supposed to be more blessed to give than to receive, most of us probably find that if our gifts strikingly exceed our receipts, or the reverse, we feel a little uncomfortable.

A very interesting but very complex example of long-run exchange is that among the generations. In any short period of time, it is clear that the people in middle life, who for the most part produce the real income of society, have to share this real income both with the young and with the old. The middle-aged must support the unproductive, whether the lack of productivity is the result of immaturity or of senescence. The problem of how much such support the middle-aged should give is always a rather critical matter of social policy, about which there may be a good deal of disagreement. This question, too, is related to the problem of interest. The property of society is mostly held by the old. If rates of interest and, indeed, rates of profit are high, the middle-aged have to contribute large amounts of the current products of society to the support of the old. If rates of interest and of profit are low, it is probable that there will be a redistribution of income away from the old, perhaps even away from the young, towards the middle-aged.

There is clearly here, something that looks like an exchange across the generations. The young are supported by the middle-aged in the hope that when the middle-aged are old, the young, who will then be middle-aged, will then support them. Thus, when we are young, we receive more than we contribute to society, in middle-age we pay off this debt, and indeed more than pay it off, by supporting both the then young and the then old. In middle-age, therefore, we not only pay off the debts of youth, but we build up a positive balance with society which we then draw upon in age. This rather idyllic picture is not, of course, always observed in practice. For society as a whole, however, it is not an unplausible description of the relations among the various age groups. In the end what looks like philanthropy often turns out to be disguised exchange—exchange, that is, over a period of years. This still does not prevent these transactions from looking very much like philanthropy in the short run.

We now come to the very interesting question of the motivation for genuinely unilateral transfers, that is, a *quid* for which there is no *quo,* not now, in the future, nor in the past. This raises the question as to whether there is anything that might be called "rational" philanthropic behavior. What are the standards, in other words, by which we can judge whether a man, or a foundation, or even a government is giving away its money wisely. It is clear that in practice we do have some standards and it therefore must make some kind of sense to talk about rational philanthropy. Philanthropic donations, that is to say, are not wholly random or arbitrary. They are capable of criticism according to some kind of welfare function even though the function may be very difficult to specify.

In a formal sense, of course, it is possible to deal with this situation by the ordinary theory of utility. We suppose that an individual or an organization has a certain amount of income to dispose of—to divide among various competing uses of which the philanthropic use is one. The formal solution to this problem is that the marginal utility of the "dollar" should be the same in all uses. Otherwise, of course, it is possible to increase the total utility by transferring dollars from one use to another. That is, we give to charity up to the point where we feel that an extra dollar given does not represent to us the same utility as a dollar devoted to other purposes, such as the purchase of commodities or the addition to our net worth. This theory is so formal that it cannot help being true. Its truth, however, does not guarantee that it should be interesting, and unless we can specify more about the nature of the utility function, this theory says very little more than: we do what we do. We may, however, at any time reexamine our mode of life and expenditure and decide that we have been putting too much in one line and not enough in another, and that hence the marginal utilities of the dollar were *not* equal—we were doing something, in other words, which on further examination proved to be irrational. It is this possibility of further examination which saves utility theory from complete emptiness. Utility theory does call our attention to the fact of cost and sacrifice and to the real nature of the problem which is involved in decisions of this sort. It saves us from notions of absolute requirements which are so congenial to the military man and to the engineer. The idea that everything has its price may expose us to the charge of cynicism but it should at least save us from the danger of a false absolutism.

Utility theory will mislead us, however, if we conclude from it that the motivation for philanthropy is no different from that for other forms of expenditure. There is nothing in this theory which suggests that all motivations are alike, even though they can be reduced formally to a single factor which we call utility. In fact, the motivation which leads to expenditure for philanthropic purposes may be very different from that which leads us to build up a personal estate or to purchase consumption goods for our own use. I refer here particularly to "genuine" donations, that is, gifts for which there is no identifiable *quid pro quo* even in the shape of a personal gratification. There is a real moral difference, I think, between the gift which is given out of vanity and the desire for self-aggrandizement or the desire to be merely fashionable, and the gift which is given out of a genuine sense of community with the object of the donation. It is this sense of community which is the essence of what I regard as genuine philanthropy. The name philanthropy, itself, which means of course, the love of man, is a clue to the essential nature of the genuine article. When we make a true gift, it is because we identify ourselves with the recipient. Even pity, which is not always a particularily ennobling virtue and which easily slips over into vanity and self-congratulation (there but for the justice of the universe, rather than the grace of God, go I!)—even pity is the manifestation of self-identification with the pitied. It is this capacity for empathy—for putting oneself in another's place, for feeling the joys and the sorrows of another as one's own—which is the source of the genuine gift. It is because "no man is an island," because the very realization of our own identity implies in some sense that there is a common identity in humanity, that we are willing to "socialize" our substance and to share with the afflicted. This is "charity" before the word became corrupted by vanity and fashion. It can be dealt with quite easily in utility theory by considering the utility of one person a function not only of his own wealth or his own income, but a function of the wealth and income of others. This assumption does not necessarily destroy the theory of exchange (as I show later), although, altruism could be carried to the point where the utility functions of two exchangers are identical over the field of possible distribution of commodities between them. In this case the parties simply move immediately to their mutual optimum in the field and whether this is done by gift or by exchange really makes very little difference. This, however, is highly unlikely. We love our neighbor, but not quite as ourselves. As he gets more and we get less, we rejoice indeed in his affluence, but at some point our dissatisfaction with our own penury is likely to exceed this vicarious enjoyment. Once we admit this fact, exchange reestablishes itself.

If we regard the philanthropic donations of an individual as an expression of his sense of community with others, a great deal that may seem mysterious or irrational about the phenomenon falls into place. Obviously, the more an individual identifies with some cause, community, or organization, the more likely he is to support it and the greater will be his donations to it. This is why the immediate face-to-face group and the reference groups with which he has identified himself always figure largely in the amounts given by an individual. When he gives to his children, for instance, he gives in a sense to an extension of himself. When he gives to a church of which he is a member, he is expressing his identity with a community a little larger than the family but fulfilling some of the same functions. As he contributes toward it, therefore, he is contributing in a sense toward part of his larger self. The larger the community, however, the harder it is to finance it by pure donations; the more tenuous the sense of identity, the less the individual feels that the community is an integral part of himself. It is a rare nation or state, therefore, that can rely on the motive of identification, that is, of genuine philanthropy for the support which it requires from its citizens. We have, therefore, the phenomenon of taxation which might be regarded as compulsory philanthropy. Baumol has pointed out that such compulsory philanthropy may be quite rational in a situation where an individual will make a contribution willingly if everybody else makes one, but would be unwilling if other people did not. Hence, an individual may advocate his own coercion simply because it is accompanied by the coercion of all the other members of the community. In large, heterogeneous, and anonymous communities in which the individual loses the sense of face-to-face contact with the other members, it is almost always necessary to reinforce philanthropy with coercion and to provide for unilateral transfers, such as taxes, under some kind of penalty for failure. Even in private communities, the threat of expulsion can be an important factor in inducing the individual to pay what looks at first sight like a purely voluntary contribution. There may, in other words, be elements of coercion even in the relationship of the individual with a purely private organization or community.

Up to now, I have been dealing mainly with the philanthropy of the individual. I now turn to the problem of the professional philanthropist, as exemplified by the foundation. We here run into a problem and a set of motivations which may be very different from those of the private individual donor. The foundation is a specialized giver. The amount which it gives is usually determined by the conditions under which it has been set up (although there may be some latitude in this regard). Consequently, its donations are not, like those of the individual giver, sharply competitive with alternative uses in consumption or in saving. Once the donor has decided to set up the foundation, the question as to how much it should give is largely taken out of the realm of decision-making. The problem of the foundation, therefore, is not so much whether its sense of community with the object of the gift merits an extra dollar drawn from competing uses, but rather, whether the money should go to one deserving object or another. The main problem of the foundation, in other words, is that of the choice among possible recipients of its bounty.

This raises the question whether we could have a theory of the foundation in the sense in which we have a theory of the firm. It is obvious that the two institutions differ sharply. The theory of profit maximization, while it is subject to many exceptions and qualifications, is at least a reasonable first approximation to the theory of the firm. We seem to have no such first approximation in the theory of the foundation. Nevertheless, a foundation must make choices much as a firm does. It has to decide that *A* is worthy and *B* is not. It must develop a policy according to which it makes and, perhaps even more important, justifies its decisions. Even though its purpose is to do good rather than to make profits and even though profits have a certain objectivity of measurement which the good has not, nevertheless, it is presumably in the interest of a foundation to do more good in its own estimation rather than less. The notion of the maximization of good, although it may not lead to a clear mathematical and objective rule of action, is at least a theoretical beginning.

A foundation faces one problem (which may also be present in the firm) in what may be an acute degree. A firm may find that it makes much the same amount of profit over a large area of its field of possible choice—in this case its actual decisions are, in a strict economic sense, indeterminate. Likewise, a foundation may come to feel that it will do about the same amount of good in widely differing areas and for widely differing distributions of its largesse among various objects. Under these circumstances, the problem of "maximizing behavior" is a very difficult one because the maximizing principle gives us no clear rule for action. It is not surprising, therefore, if organizations develop rules of thumb or what might be called rules of exclusion. A wide and open field gives us agoraphobia. We therefore build fences across it and around it. We say we will not do *A*, we will not do *B*, we will not do *C* and by the time we have excluded these possibilities by rule, there may be only one alternative left to us, *D*, which we then select. One can see this happening constantly in the foundations—one of the first decisions that a board of directors of a foundation makes is what it will *not* do. It partitions the general field and almost always decides to limit itself to a small area.

The process of decision-making by successive elimination is, of course, not confined to foundations. Every individual, organization, or society, when absolute rationality, that is, "maximizing" behavior is despaired of, retreats into taboo, ritual and rule of thumb. There is, perhaps, more excuse for this kind of behavior in the foundation than there is in many other forms of organization. Even in the foundation, however, it frequently represents a retreat from responsibility. An organization which follows this principle also is in grave danger of finding its principles obsolete. The world is apt to change more rapidly than our rules about it. A foundation which decided, for instance, to support only a particular area of medical research might find itself left high and dry when this particular area encounters success.

Even though it is very difficult to specify the exact form of the welfare function of a foundation, there is a certain analog of the market in the mutual competition of foundations for grantees and of potential grantees for foundation support. There is even a certain analogy between the "states of the market" as we develop this in the theory of monopoly and imperfect competition and the various possible states of the relations between foundations and their grantees. We can visualize the situation, for instance, of extreme monopoly of the granting power. The totalitarian socialist state would be such a monopoly. Here the success of a potential grantee depends upon his ability to present his case before the right persons and the right channels within the monolithic organization of the granting power. By contrast, suppose a situation analogous to perfect competition in which there are a large number of foundations and a large number of grantees. Here there is a possibility of shopping around. An applicant who is unsuccessful with one foundation may turn to another and vice versa. There is in fact some competition among the foundations for desirable applicants, but ordinarily we may assume that the amount which applicants are seeking is very much in excess of what the foundations are able and willing to grant. Hence, the rationing function has to be performed by the foundation rather than by the applicant.

It would be very interesting if we could develop theorems relating the state of the granting market in regard to monopoly or competition to the desirability of the results and if we could, for instance, make a case against monopoly of the granting power, as we can make a case against monopoly in exchange relationships. I have an intuitive feeling that some such proposition is plausible. I would not be so presumptuous, however, as to attempt to demonstrate it. We need in the first place, some measure of the success of the granting program. What is it, in other words, that would make one distribution of grants among the potential applicants better or worse than another such distribution? Strong cases can easily be cited. The Ford Foundation, for instance, is rarely blamed even by its most vociferous critics for rejecting a proposal to plant a 3,000-mile-long rose garden along the frontier of the United States and Canada as a symbol, or perhaps as a memorial, to the peaceful relations established along this border. Once we leave the patently absurd, however, there seems to be room for strong differences of opinion as to the wise course to follow in the making of grants. The rejected suitors naturally feel hurt and indignant. Foundations may tend to minimize this hurt by giving everybody a little. This seems, indeed, to have been the principle of The Ford Foundation. It is subject to the criticism that it results in a large number of weak proposals and weak institutions instead of a few strong ones. It is arguable, for instance, that Rockefeller did more for American education, even for the salaries of professors, by establishing a single strong University of Chicago than The Ford Foundation has done by broadcasting its largesse.

The problem of the ideal structure of foundation grants is complicated by the fact that the effects of these grants are often not what either the donor or the recipient intend. This is mainly owing to the varying elasticities in the supply of labor, especially intellectual labor. When a grant is given for a certain purpose, the assumption is that there exists a market within which the accomplishment of this purpose can be bought. If in fact, a supply of whatever it is that embodies the purpose is highly inelastic, the main result of the grant will be to bid up the price of this supply rather than to increase its quantity. In the long run, of course, if the grant is repeated and continuous, supplies tend to be more elastic. Most foundation grants, however, do not operate in the long run. Thus, if a number of foundations start giving grants for, shall we say, studies in Chinese, the main result is to bid up the price of Chinese specialists, sometimes to the point where the traditional structure of incomes is seriously disturbed, and yet there is not much increase in the total body of Chinese studies produced. The competing programs spend most of their time, energy, and money in bidding the specialists away from each other.

Just as we used what might be called the principle of reexamination to rescue the theory of utility from total formalism, so we might invoke the same principle in the theory of grants. A foundation may certainly regret having made a grant and an applicant may even regret having received it; there may be afterthoughts and reexaminations. One of the institutional problems, therefore, is the learning process by which the foundations and other granting agencies learn from their mistakes. One difficulty here in attempting to use the analogy of competition is that in a market situation, especially in perfect competition, a firm which makes serious mistakes will go out of existence. The only fatal mistakes which a foundation can make, however, are in its investment policy, not in its granting policy. As far as I can see, there is nothing in social ecology which would lead to the elimination of a foundation which indulged in the uttermost folly in its grant-making, provided that its investment policy was sound. Foolish or irresponsible grant-making might, of course, in the long run stir up enough social resentment to lead to the disestablishment of the foundations. The dissolution of the monasteries stands as a solemn historical warning. The presence of immortals is always an embarrassment to a mortal society, and it is certainly easy to imagine that the foundations might become such large and significant centers of private power that the state will be forced to disestablish them. This follows from the position of the foundation as an element in the polity rather than in the economy. The prospect of disestablishment in the future, however, is little safeguard against mistakes in the present.

By way of conclusion, if the case for competition among foundations is a strong one, one wonders whether there is not also a case for something like an antitrust law for foundations. The very large foundations do represent a source of political and economic power, which however wisely exercised, is politically irresponsible; that is, not responsible to anybody beyond a self-perpetuating body of trustees. A situation like this in a society always contains the seeds of potential danger. A law which would compel the split of any foundation exceeding perhaps $100,000,000 would at least distribute this power more widely, would lessen the possibility of really disastrous mistakes, and would give the applicant a better chance to shop around. Even a superficial knowledge of the activities of foundations suggests that it is the small ones which are frequently the most creative and imaginative. The larger a foundation gets, the more it begins to look like an arm of government and the less justification there seems to be, therefore, for the private exercise of this power.

Appendix: Altruism and Utility

The theory of exchange or bilateral monopoly, as developed in the first instance by Edgeworth, can easily be adapted to any degree of altruism that we wish. In the usual exposition, we indicate the distribution of two commodities between two exchangers by the position of a point P inside the box O_aXO_bY—O_a being the point where exchanger A has none of either commodity, and O_b the point where exchanger B has no commodity. O_aX is the total amount of commodity X and O_aY is the total amount of commodity Y to be divided between the two exchangers. Thus at the point P, exchanger A has Y_aP of commodity X and PX_a of commodity Y; exchanger B has PY_b of commodity Y and PX_b of commodity X. In pure exchange, of course, there is no change in the total quantity of the two commodities. Exchange is merely a rearrangement of assets.

In the usual analysis, we suppose that each party to the exchange has a utility function represented by indifference curves—the solid curved lines being those for A, the broken lines being those for B (see Figure 1). We suppose that A's utility increases the more he has of anything and the less B has, and B's utility increases the more he has and the less A has. This is the usual nonaltruistic case. If we visualize the utility functions in the third dimension above the plane of the paper, A's utility function is a mountain which rises continuously as we go away from O_a in any direction. B's utility function is a mountain which rises likewise as we go away from O_b in any direction. The heavy dotted line $C_1C_2C_3$ is the contract curve or the locus of the points of tangency of the two systems of indifference curves. It is easy to show that from any point in the figure not on the con-

FIGURE 1

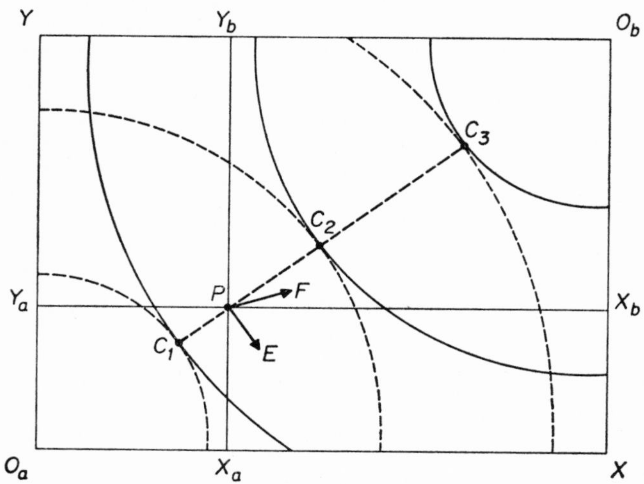

tract curve, it is possible to reach points on the contract curve by some process of exchange which will make both parties better off.

In the ordinary case, *A*'s utility depends only on the amounts of commodity which he possesses, and similarly for *B*. There is no reason, however, why we should not extend the analysis to include the case in which *A*'s utility depends not only on what he has, but also on what *B* has. In this case, we might suppose that *A*'s total utility consists of two parts—the part which is derived from his own possession of the two commodities and the part which is derived from his contemplation of *B*'s possession of them, that is, from altruism. Thus, suppose we take a section of the three-dimensional utility surfaces along the line Y_aX_b (see Figure 2), where utility is measured in the vertical direction. We may suppose that Y_aU_a represents the direct utility to *A* of the increase in commodity *X*. The curve X_bU_b represents the indirect utility to *A* as he contemplates *B* increasing the amount of commodity *X* which *B* possesses. The sum of these two utility curves is the curve $U_bU_mU_a$. We are assuming here, of course, all sorts of shocking things about the measurability and comparability of utilities, but this may be unavoidable.

In Figure 3, we return to the axes of Figure 1 and draw the indifference curves of the two parties which would correspond to the utility functions of Figure 2. The solid lines, as before, represent the indiffer-

FIGURE 2

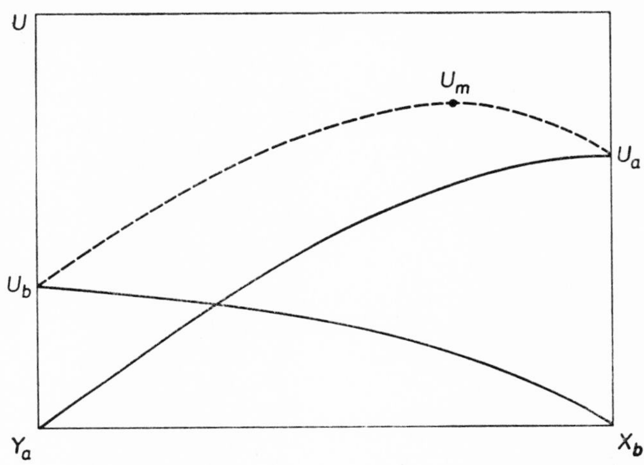

ence curves of party A and the dotted lines of party B. It will be observed that the corresponding utility functions now exhibit a maximum at M_a and M_b respectively. This means that as we move from M_a toward O_b, A's utility actually declines, in spite of the fact that he is gaining more goods, because the direct gain to himself is outweighed by the pity which he feels at B's miserable poverty. Similarly, B's utility declines as we move from M_b toward O_a.

Consider now, the line $H_aM_aK_a$ which is drawn through all the points where A's indifference curves are vertical, and the corresponding line $L_aM_aN_a$ which is drawn through all the points where A's indifference curves are horizontal. These lines, intersecting at M_a, divide the field into four regions. In the region $O_aH_aM_aL_a$, A's indifference curves are the same as in Figure 1, that is to say, he is selfish in both commodities. In the region $M_aN_aO_aK_a$, he is altruistic in both commodities. It is impossible, formally, to distinguish this case from the case where the commodities have become discommodities, but in our case, we suppose they have become discommodities to A because of his altruism. He cannot bear to have more of them at B's expense. In the region $L_aM_aK_aX$, he is selfish in regard to commodity Y and altruistic in regard to commodity X. This situation is exactly reversed in the area $H_aM_aN_aY$. Similar lines, $H_bM_bK_b$ and $L_bM_bN_b$, can be drawn through M_b and a similar analysis performed for the party B. These two sets of lines divide the field into nine regions. To avoid further confusion in the figure, we number these from one to nine

FIGURE 3

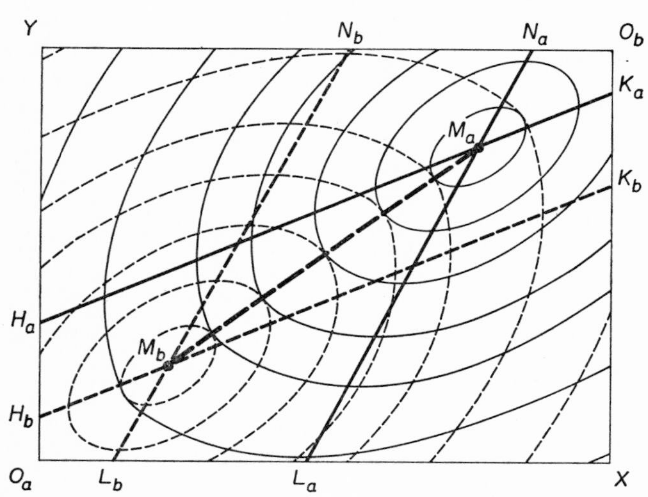

FIGURE 4

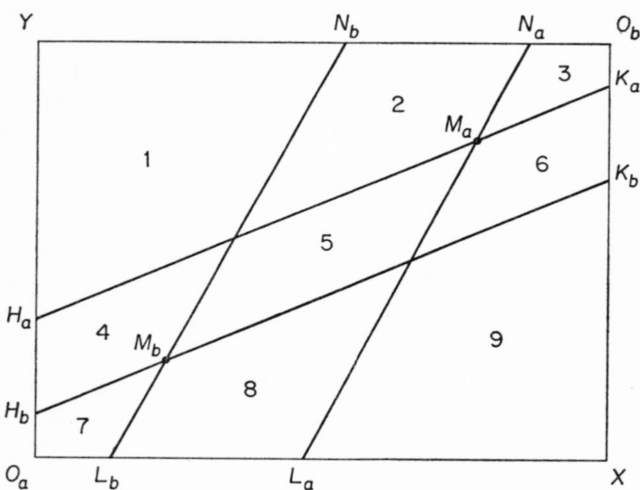

in Figure 4. In the central region, 5, both parties are selfish in both commodities. The situation is essentially the same as in Figure 1. The contract curve joins M_b to M_a and the analysis of exchange follows exactly as it does in Figure 1. In region 7, *A* is selfish and *B* is altruistic in both commodities. Exchange is impossible from any point within the region. *B* will simply give *A* both commodities until the point M_b is reached. This is, therefore, a region of two-commodity philanthropy for *B*. Similarly, the region labeled 3 is a region of two-commodity philanthropy for *A*, and from any point in this region, we proceed immediately to M_a. Regions 2, 4, 6, and 8 are characterized by the fact that each party is altruistic in one commodity and selfish in another, and that the commodity in which one party is altruistic will be that in which the other party is selfish. In region 1, both parties are altruistic in *X* and selfish in *Y*; in region 9, both parties are altruistic in *Y* and selfish in *X*.

We see in this figure that both exchange and philanthropy are special cases of movement within the field of the figure. Exchange is a movement in any direction on a line with a negative but not infinite slope, such as for instance, *PE* in Figure 1. Here each party gives up one commodity to the other and receives the other commodity in return. A horizontal movement is a pure gift of commodity *X*, thus a movement from *P* toward X_b in Figure 1 is a gift of commodity *X* from *A* to *B*. A movement from *P* to Y_a is a gift of commodity *X* from *B* to *A*. Similarly a vertical move in either direction is a gift of commodity *Y*. A move along a line with a positive slope, such as *PF* in Figure 1, represents a gift of both commodities. If we define a "trading move" as a move which makes both parties better off than they were before, we see that, in region 5, only exchanges can be trading moves. In regions 1 and 9, both exchanges and gifts of both commodities by either party in certain proportions can be trading moves. In regions 7 and 3, exchanges cannot be trading moves. In regions 2, 4, 6 and 8, exchange may be a trading move, and gifts of the two commodities in certain proportions by only one of the parties may also be trading moves.

In the case of total altruism, where each party regards the interest of the other as identical with his own, the points M_a and M_b move together until they coincide. When this happens, regions 2, 4, 5, 6 and 8 disappear. Both parties will move towards a single optimum, either by exchange in regions 1 and 9 or by gifts of both commodities in regions 3 and 7. It is interesting to note that even in this extreme case, exchange is not wholly ruled out; but, of course, the contract curve shrinks to a single point and there is no conflict.

Hospitals and Philanthropy

Eli Ginzberg
Columbia University

Introduction

The amount and proportion that philanthropy contributes to the income of institutions performing essential community services are likely to change in response to a great number of factors: in particular, alterations in the size and distribution of the national income, the nature of the services and their cost structures, alterations in the mechanisms available for financing various services, changes in the role of government, and shifts in social values. Each of these determinants has altered, to some degree and at some time, the role of philanthropy in the financing of general hospital care in the United States during the past half century.

To set the stage for the analysis which follows it may be helpful to note briefly the order of change which has taken place in the economy at large during the past fifty years. There has been a substantial rise in per capita real income in the United States and there has been a faster than average gain for those at the bottom of the income scale. The amount and proportion of income available for discretionary use beyond expenditures for food, clothing, and rent have likewise increased substantially.

It was not until after World War I that the general hospital became an institution basic to the medical care of the entire community rather than one catering primarily to the indigent poor. It was not until the 1920's that the majority of babies were delivered in hospitals. I personally recall that my sister's tonsils were extracted on the kitchen table in 1920 with our family physician acting as the anesthetist. And we lived in New York City!

The trend in hospital costs can be briefly summarized. The per diem cost increased from between $4 and $5 in 1929 to $30 in 1960.[1] Eliminating the inflationary element, per diem costs in real terms advanced in the last thirty years by a factor of two to three.

The Great Depression saw the beginnings of the Blue Cross system, a prepayment insurance device for meeting hospital bills; and some years later Blue Shield made its appearance—a comparable insurance system for the prepayment of physicians' services rendered patients in hospitals. By 1960 the numbers enrolled in these two nonprofit plans, together with those enrolled in related commercial insurance plans, began to approximate the total potential enrollees among the working members of the population and their dependents.

After the Great Depression there was a major shift in the extent to which government was forced to assume financial responsibility in providing for the maintenance and emergency needs of the indigent and near-indigent members of the community. And since the end of World War II, government has entered upon, through the Hill-Burton Act, a large-scale grant program for the construction, and more recently for the remodelling, of hospital and related facilities.

Finally, the public's contributions for philanthropic purposes have fluctuated in amount and more particularly in the way they have been distributed. In 1929–30, income per patient day in voluntary general hospitals in New York State amounted to slightly more than $4 of which charity contributed $2. Three years later the contribution of philanthropy had dropped to 84 cents.[2] But there occurred a substantial increase in government payments for public charges. The Great Depression marked the watershed: before it, philanthropy devoted much of its funds to buying essential commodities and services for those unable to purchase them; after it, meeting the basic budget of the indigent came to be viewed as the primary responsibility of government.[3]

Some other important and relevant trends are: changes in personal income tax policy with consequences for the proportion of hospital

[1] Eli Ginzberg, *A Pattern for Hospital Care,* New York, 1949, p. 134; American Hospital Association: *Hospital Rates 1959,* Chicago, 1960, p. 15; and *Daily Service Charges in Hospitals, 1960,* Chicago, 1961, p. 4.

[2] *A Pattern for Hospital Care,* p. 135.

[3] Thomas Karter, "Voluntary Agency Expenditures for Health and Welfare from Philanthropic Contributions, 1930–55" in *Social Security Bulletin,* February 1958, p. 2.

costs carried by the patient; new patterns of community fund raising which have tapped additional sources of philanthropic support; the much deeper involvement of hospitals in educational functions; changes in hospital utilization patterns; and other developments that have altered radically the hospital's cost and income structure. The main purpose in this presentation is to identify and evaluate the major forces that have brought the hospital from the periphery of the market economy into the center. For today, expenditures in *non-federal* hospitals providing short-term care total over $5 billion annually.

The U.S. Hospital System

The United States has a dual system of hospital care—one that has been long established and that, despite minor alterations, shows every evidence of basic stability. Government hospitals primarily provide care for patients suffering from mental or other chronic diseases; private hospitals, primarily for patients requiring short-term care.

Despite this basic duality there is an indistinct area. The federal government provides a considerable amount of short-term care in its own hospitals for special groups such as military personnel, veterans, Indians, and merchant seamen. State, county, and local governments, particularly the last two, provide considerable short-term care for both paying and indigent patients in hospitals which they own and operate. All units of government also pay for the hospitalization of various individuals for whom they are responsible when such individuals are treated in hospitals other than those which they operate. In recent years a growing number of the larger nonprofit hospitals have begun to provide short-term psychiatric care; and a few major teaching hospitals operate modest tuberculosis services, also for short-term patients. Despite these and other overlappings, the two are distinct systems and are likely to remain so.

The current pattern of hospital care can be briefly summarized by type of hospitals and type of beds. Of a total of approximately 6,800 hospitals (1958) government operated more than 2,200: the federal government 400, state governments about 550, and local government over 1,250.

Of the almost 1.6 million total beds, government hospitals accounted for by far the largest proportion: hospitals operated by the federal and local governments had slightly less than 200,000 each and state governments about 700,000. The nation's 1,000 proprietary hospitals controlled less than 50,000 beds, and the 3,500 nonprofit hospitals (church and other) were responsible for approximately 460,000 beds.

Disregarding the 65,000 beds for tuberculosis patients and 75,000 beds used for patients with other specialized conditions, the bulk of all hospital beds are divided more or less evenly between those provided for patients requiring general hospital care and those for patients suffering from nervous and mental diseases.[4]

With approximately equal numbers of beds, mental hospitals admit during the course of a year under 300,000 patients, while general hospitals admit over 21 million! The maintenance cost of caring for a mental patient averages about $4 to $5 per day. The per diem cost for a patient in a general hospital today approximates $30. Clearly the two systems differ not only as to ownership and type of patient treated but also with respect to the range of services provided and the costs involved.

In 1956–57 the United States spent approximately $6.4 billion on all types of hospital care (depreciation and the administrative costs of hospital insurance excluded). Government covered 40 per cent; private sources, including philanthropy, 60 per cent. About 79 per cent of all expenditures were in general short-term hospitals, the remainder primarily in psychiatric (17 per cent) and in tuberculosis hospitals (4 per cent).

Of the approximately $2.5 billion spent by government, the federal government accounted for slightly more than $1 billion, three-quarters of which was spent for general hospital care. Of the almost $1.5 billion spent by state and local governments, half was for the care of patients with mental disease, two-fifths for general hospital care, and the remaining one-tenth for care of patients suffering from tuberculosis.

The almost $4 billion income from private sources was distributed as follows: about $3 billion in short-term private hospitals and a half billion in public hospitals for general hospital care. The remainder, slightly under $300 million, was spent for care of mental, tubercular, and other long-term chronic patients.[5]

Several generalizations can now be made about the role of philanthropy in the financing of hospital care in the United States. Philanthropy plays almost no role in the support of public hospitals, which account for only a little less than half of all expenditures for hospital

[4] *Statistical Abstract of the United States,* 1960, p. 76.

[5] "Public and Private Expenditures for Hospital Care in the United States, 1956–57," *Research and Statistics Note No. 19,* July 10, 1959, Social Security Administration, U.S. Department of Health, Education, and Welfare.

care. Since public hospitals provide most of the care for mental patients, philanthropy makes little contribution to the care of this significant group of patients. Clearly there is no role for philanthropy in proprietary hospitals. The philanthropic effort in the field of hospital care is therefore predominantly concentrated in nonprofit, short-term hospitals. For this reason, this analysis will seek to trace, primarily, the changing relations between philanthropy and short-term nonfederal hospitals.

Philanthropy's Role in Financing Short-Term Nonfederal Hospitals

Reference was made earlier to the fact that philanthropy accounted for almost half of the patient income received by general hospitals in New York State in 1929. This single fact underscores the very considerable role that philanthropy played in hospital financing, at least in one section of the country, as recently as the onset of the Great Depression.

The first reliable national estimate is of a later date, 1935, a year for which the U.S. Public Health Service, making use of Census data, developed the basic data. Dr. Herbert Klarman, Associate Director of the Hospital Council of Greater New York, is responsible for the preparation of comparable data for later years (1950 and 1958) and for incisive analyses of philanthropy's share in the financing of nonprofit general hospitals.

In 1935 the total income of short-term nonfederal hospitals was about $448 million. Philanthropy contributed $60 million for roughly 13 per cent of the total. Government's share was over $106 million or about 24 per cent of the total. Private payments of $282 million accounted for more than three-fifths of the total.

A review of the 1950 data reveals that the total income of these hospitals had increased almost fivefold—to over $2.2 billion. The absolute amount contributed by philanthropy had increased substantially, from $60 to $155 million, but because of the much greater increase in total income, philanthropy's share had declined by almost half—from 13.4 per cent to 7.0 per cent.

During the fifteen years from 1935 to 1950 there was a decline of 3.0 percentage points in the proportion covered by tax funds which, together with the decline of 6.4 percentage points in philanthropy's proportion, resulted in a 9.4 per cent increase in the proportion covered by private sources. By 1950, private sources had come to account for almost three-quarters of the total income of short-term nonfederal hospitals.

The figures for 1958 revealed the continuation of this trend. Total income of nonfederal short-term hospitals had increased to almost $4.8 billion—more than double that of 1950. Philanthropy's total climbed again, reaching $226 million, an increase of $111 million in eight years. But the relative share of philanthropy declined in these years; it now represented only 4.7 per cent of total income, a decline of 2.3 percentage points in eight years. In the 1950's, the relative role of tax funds in the financing of these short-term hospitals dropped strikingly. In 1958 the $666 million contributed by government accounted for 13.7 per cent of the total—a decline of 6.0 percentage points from 1950.[6]

These selective data indicate that the period since 1935 has witnessed a major revolution in the financing of general hospital care. At the beginning of the period patients paid for only slightly more than three-fifths of the total hospital bill. The remainder was covered by government and philanthropy, the latter accounting for approximately one-seventh of the total. Twenty-three years later the individual patient, either through direct payments or through insurance, was covering almost 82 per cent of the total bill. By 1958, philanthropy paid for only about one-twentieth instead of one-seventh of the cost of general hospital care.

During this period the total income of general hospitals had increased more than tenfold. While philanthropic contributions had climbed from $60 to $226 million annually, the rate of increase lagged far behind that in total income.

Further perspective on the significance of philanthropy in financing general hospital care can be obtained by estimating the number of patients whose hospital bill could have been covered by charitable contributions. In 1957 there were just over 21 million patients admitted to general hospitals. Since philanthropy accounted for 4.2 per cent of all general hospital income, the entire cost of the hospitalization of about 900,000 patients might have been covered by charity.

But in point of fact the use of the philanthropic dollar was at once broader and narrower. A considerable part of all charitable contributions was spent as always on important hospital functions that are only indirectly connected with services to inpatients. These in-

[6] *Geographic Comparison in Financing Hospital Care,* Hospital Council of Greater New York, vol. 15, No. 3, New York, 1960.

clude the support of education and research; and underpinning the finances of ancillary departments, such as social service, rehabilitation, and home care. Then, too, a considerable number of general hospitals, especially in large metropolitan centers, operate sizeable outpatient departments which frequently run substantial deficits. This suggests that the cost of hospitalizing considerably fewer than 900,000 inpatients was covered by philanthropy.

But there are factors which indicate that much larger numbers profit to some degree from philanthropy's contribution. In terms of the quality of care received, the number can be said to be identical with the sum of all in- and outpatients, for the level of hospital services is always somewhat higher by virtue of the additional dollars made available by philanthropy.

There is a further factor: few hospitals use their philanthropic funds to cover hospitalization costs of individuals who are without financial resources. Those at the bottom of the income scale are most likely to be public charges and, as such, are likely to have their hospital expenses paid for by government. But these government payments seldom cover the hospital's total cost. Many other patients are also able to pay only part of their total bill. Thus, the amount of philanthropic funds enables a hospital to determine how much "free care" it is able to provide; free care here is defined as the hospital's contribution where payment is less than cost.

In 1958 the per diem income from ward patients in nine selected general hospitals in New York City—a community in which philanthropy still looms relatively large in the provision of hospital care—was about $18. The per diem cost was about $28—assuming, as is reasonable, that the per diem cost for ward patients was not lower than for most other patients. There was thus a loss of about $10 per ward patient. Without entering upon refined calculations involving such matters as a greater-than-average length of stay for ward patients and differences between marginal and average costs, we can say that the typical ward patient was subsidized to an amount of approximately $100. On this basis we can say also that the total philanthropic contribution helped over 2 million patients meet their costs of hospitalization. While this is a significant figure, even more important is the fact that 19 million patients treated in general hospitals thus received no direct financial help from the sums contributed by philanthropy.[7]

[7] Eli Ginzberg and Peter Rogatz, *Planning for Better Hospital Care,* New York, 1961, p. 64.

Types of Philanthropic Contributions

The data relating to philanthropy presented above have included only contributions in money to the operating budget of general hospitals and the earnings on unrestricted endowments. While these two categories probably account for most of the philanthropic support which hospitals receive, it would be well to consider the entire range of charitable contributions available to nonprofit hospitals.

Hospitals have long practiced price discrimination in that they have charged different rates for different types of accommodations. Without clear-cut economic justification, they charge noticeably less for ward than for semiprivate accommodations and noticeably more for private than for semiprivate. While the growth of Blue Cross and other forms of hospital insurance has put pressure on hospitals to rationalize their costs and charges—at least to relate their charges for semiprivate accommodations to average costs—many institutions with sizeable sources of philanthropic income have tended to keep their ward rates considerably below average costs and private rates considerably in excess, although presumably a detailed cost analysis would not justify such differentials. If anything, ward costs in a teaching hospital are probably higher than in either semiprivate or private accommodations because of the substantial volume of diagnostic procedures ordered freely by interns and residents and the associated high use of drugs and nursing and other services.

It is not difficult, however, to understand why this practice of price discrimination has been continued. Many voluntary hospitals have long taken pride in providing care for the poor and indigent at no charge or at a charge considerably below cost. Likewise hospitals have had little hesitancy in extracting what is tantamount to a charitable contribution from those sufficiently wealthy to prefer private accommodations.

The nine general hospitals in New York City which were earlier described as losing an average of about $10 a patient day on the wards averaged a per diem income from private accommodations of about $17 above their average costs. But the income derived from private patients accounted for only about 15 per cent of all income from inpatients, which indicates that even under a highly discriminatory pricing policy the yield from this forced contribution is modest.[8]

For the country as a whole, private accommodations account for

[8] *Ibid.*

only between one-fifth and one-fourth of all beds in nonprofit short-term hospitals. Moreover, a comparison between the average rates for these accommodations and average costs suggests that the pattern prevailing in the New York City voluntary hospitals is atypical; most hospitals did not make a substantial profit from patients in private accommodations.

A review of the percentage changes in daily charges between 1948 and 1960 by type of accommodations—single, two bed and multiple—fails to reveal any significant differences in the rates of increases among these three classes. Apparently nonprofit hospitals did not attempt to charge all that the traffic would bear for private accommodations. They were probably inhibited first by a fear that their charge structure would be out of line with other hospitals. But more importantly, because they were forced to advance their average charges steadily, and by large increments, which in itself resulted in considerable community criticism, there was strong pressure against a further increase in private charges, even though the profit on such charges might have covered the losses on ward patients. Finally, many less affluent patients were frequently forced, because of their medical condition or because of a shortage of semiprivate accommodations, to accept private accommodations. This made it undesirable to extract a forced contribution from this group.

While data are not available to develop a sound estimate of the size of the "forced contribution" that nonprofit hospitals extract from private patients, a first approximation can be ventured. In 1958 voluntary short-term hospitals received in patient payments approximately $3.1 billion. If between one-fifth and one-fourth of their total accommodations consisted of single bed units, and a profit of around 10 per cent on these accommodations is presumed, their total gain from this source would have been approximately $65 million. Dr. Klarman's estimates for New York City for 1957–58 show a net gain from private accommodations amounting to about 1.2 per cent of the total income of all nonfederal general care hospitals, a figure which would yield a total sum of over $57 million for the entire country.[9] The significance of this sum can best be appreciated when it is placed against "total" philanthropic contributions for operating purposes of about $200 million for the same year.

The biggest factor in hospital operating expenses has long been wages and salaries; today this segment accounts for about two-thirds

[9] Herbert Klarman, *Hospital Care in New York City: The Roles of Voluntary and Municipal Hospitals,* New York, 1962.

of all costs. The overriding importance of personnel expenditures makes it desirable, therefore, to consider developments in this sector that may have a bearing on the role of philanthropy in hospital financing.

There are several points worth noting. First, many hospitals have long been engaged not only in treating the sick and injured but also in training physicians, nurses, and other medical personnel. For several decades hospitals with nurses' training schools made a profit from this facet of their operations. For room, board, and a modest amount of didactic instruction (much of which was provided free of charge by the members of the visiting medical staff), the hospital received the labor of student nurses for three years. After World War II, for many reasons, nursing education was reformed—at least at the better institutions. The primary objective of the revised three- and four-year programs was the education of the student nurse, not the extraction of free labor. As a consequence of this reform many hospitals found that instead of making a gain, or at least breaking even on the operation of a school of nursing, they actually lost money, possibly $1,000 or more per annum per trainee.

Something else happened on the nursing front. During the depressed 1930's many hospitals, by offering nurses room, board, and a very modest monthly salary, were able to expand their staffs substantially. Not only were nurses willing to work for very little but they put in very long days; it was common practice for them to work split shifts. As happened to many institutional employees, wage and salary adjustments lagged during the war and postwar inflation. For many years, hospitals profited from delays in salary and wage adjustments. The last few years, however, have seen belated corrections and improvements. It could be said that before these occurred, hospitals were able to force a significant "charitable" contribution from their nursing staffs.

To a marked degree this has also been true of other hospital personnel. Outside of the protection of labor legislation, and usually without the help that comes from union organization, many service personnel have worked for wages far below the minimum prevailing in the profit sector of the economy. In fact, the hospitals have long attracted many persons with little skill. Having attracted and hired them, the hospitals failed to help them acquire the range of skills which would justify their being paid at a higher rate. It was little short of scandalous to find employees of major voluntary hospitals in New York City in 1959 earning $32 or $35 weekly. Here too, many hospitals have succeeded in extracting a "philanthropic" contribution.

The physician is the backbone of the system of hospital care. In addition to training nurses, most of the larger and many of the smaller hospitals have also become involved in the postgraduate training of physicians. For many decades the hospital's responsibility in this regard was limited to the formal training of interns, but in more recent years many institutions have also become engaged in the training of residents. More than half of all young physicians now complete a period of residency which requires a minimum of three and more frequently four or even five years of hospital training beyond internship.

Historically internship was apprentice training. The young physician lived in the hospital and in return for room, board, laundry, and, if lucky, $25 a month, the hospital had complete command over his time and energies seven days and six nights a week. This was a three-cornered arrangement. The intern learned from the attending staff (and from the nurses). The hospital received his services for very little; the senior staff were able to increase the number of ward and private patients whom they treated.

Since World War II the old pattern of postgraduate education of physicians has been greatly altered, and this has had serious financial consequences for the hospital. Major teaching hospitals have been forced to add a considerable number of full-time senior staff to provide the supervision and instruction required for the training of large numbers of interns and residents. Moreover, young physicians no longer live in the hospital; they are married and are fathers. Because they now work a regular day shift, many hospitals have been forced to hire and pay other physicians to insure coverage at night. Finally, many costly diagnostic and therapeutic procedures are carried out more for the educational advantage of the young physician than for the benefit of the patient with resulting upward pressure on hospital costs.

In brief, the teaching hospital has been forced to accommodate itself to a loss of much free or underpaid labor over the past two decades; and, to make its financial position worse, it has had to incur many additional expenses as a result of its expanded and improved educational efforts. It has compensated for this, in considerable measure, by putting its educational costs into its rate base; thus patients (including those with insurance) assume the cost. Here, then, is another type of forced contribution.

While it is generally true that the patients treated in large teaching hospitals are likely to receive better than average care, the fact remains that because of inadequacies in the public and private financing of the education of nurses and physicians, the private patient, with or without Blue Cross or other systems of hospital insurance, is forced to contribute, through the payment of higher charges, what may approximate an "overcharge" of $150 million. Assuming that one-third of all general hospitalization is provided in institutions with broad teaching programs and assuming that such programs add only 10 per cent to the average bill, a figure in excess of $150 million per annum would result.

Passing note should be taken of still other types of philanthropic contributions. There are the donated services of sisters, primarily in Catholic hospitals. The United Hospital Fund in New York City estimated that in 1958 the value of these donated services amounted to almost $1.6 million. While there is no ready basis for calculating the total value of the services donated by Catholic sisters throughout the United States, it is surely a sum many times greater than for New York City alone.

Nonprofit hospitals still rely heavily on the work of volunteers. Not only do volunteers raise considerable sums for operating and capital programs, they also have various managerial and service functions. Moreover, women's auxiliaries frequently devote much time to the supplemental care of patients and to special activities, such as the operation of the gift shop which frequently adds to the hospital's total income.

In addition, in recent years the patient's family has come to serve as an auxiliary labor force in many hospitals, helping to fill the gap resulting from a shortage of nurses and ancillary service personnel. I have pointed out in other connections that, since there is little prospect that this country will ever train or pay for all the nurses needed, we must look forward to relying more on this family-labor reserve. While there is no ready way of calculating the monetary value of the work of volunteers and members of patients' families, there is every reason to believe that it is a substantial sum.[10]

Reference must also be made to additional "contributions" even if they cannot be readily subsumed under philanthropy. Nonprofit hospitals continue to receive a considerable amount of donations in kind from pharmaceutical and other medical supply companies; and

[10] *Employment, Growth, and Price Levels,* Hearings before Joint Economic Committee, 86th Congress, 1st session, Part 8, pp. 2661 ff.

they also benefit from special discounts on many items that they purchase.[11]

More important, nonprofit hospitals are exempt from taxation. The question has been raised as to the justification of this if hospitals further reduce or eliminate free care to indigent patients—the original basis for their preferred tax status.

Finally, most hospitals have until recently excluded depreciation in their cost accounting. This frequently results in charges to many patients below the total of their true costs. While many who profit from this situation later contribute to the hospital's capital campaign for renovation or expansion, others do not. These last benefit from philanthropy, whether or not they are in need.

The burden of this analysis is clear. The $200 million estimated as the current philanthropic contribution to voluntary hospitals represents only one segment of a much larger flow of "contributions" in money, kind, and service all of which warrant consideration if the economics of hospital financing is to be properly appraised. Among the most important of these supplementary items are the overcharges to private patients, the unrequited services of physicians, nurses, and volunteers, and the special advantages that flow from tax exemption. Together these items have a net value considerably in excess of the dollar volume of philanthropic contributions.

Regional Variations in Philanthropic Contributions

While it is illuminating to deal with national totals, a fuller understanding of the role of philanthropy in hospital financing requires a consideration of regional and local variations. The philanthropic funds available to one hospital cannot be used to cover the operating deficit of another. And, as we shall see, great variations exist among hospitals in different regions and localities as to the philanthropic sums at their disposal.

Tradition plays an important part in the philanthropic effort devoted to hospitals. Several of the teaching hospitals along the eastern seaboard—in Boston, New York, Philadelphia, Baltimore—have roots that go back to the eighteenth century. Their ability to teach was intimately connected with their philanthropic resources; that is, their free funds enabled them to care for the poor and the indigent, and the ward patient provided, and still largely provides, these institutions

11 *Corporate Contributions to Hospitals,* National Better Business Bureau, Inc., New York, 1955.

with their basic teaching material.[12] Various religious and ethnic groups have long raised considerable sums for the support of hospitals under their control, originally to take care of their poor confreres, more recently to provide superior hospital services and educational opportunities and to discharge broader communal responsibilities. Finally, there are communities, largely in the east but also in the middle west and the west, where substantial sums are raised locally for the support of voluntary hospitals under nonsectarian auspices.

The New York State Hospital Study, which I directed in 1948, revealed a marked variation in the proportion of funds for general hospital care provided by philanthropy in New York City and in the principal cities of upstate New York. In New York City, philanthropy accounted for just under 9 per cent of total income; in the four major upstate cities the corresponding figure ranged from a low of 2.4 to a high of 3.7. We also discovered at that time that a relatively small number of hospitals in New York City received the bulk of all philanthropic funds.[13]

Recent analyses by Dr. Klarman indicate that the earlier findings have not been significantly altered by the passage of time. Nine out of the sixty-two general-care member hospitals of the United Hospital Fund in New York City received half of all cash contributions. This amounted to about $14.5 million in 1958, including those contributions made available to hospitals through central collecting agencies. Furthermore, three-quarters of the more than $7 million income available for general purposes from investments was concentrated in that year among eight of the sixty-two hospitals.[14]

So much for the striking variations within one large community in which philanthropy plays a disproportionately large role. What about regional differences? Klarman recently completed (1959) a special questionnaire study which yielded some illuminating new information. He had useful replies from fifteen large cities out of an original sample of seventeen. In contrast to New York City where philanthropy accounted for 7.1 per cent of the estimated income of short-term hospitals, the percentage for the fifteen large cities was only 3.4, less than half of the New York figure. A more detailed analysis revealed that there was a significant regional variation: in the eight east coast cities

[12] Nathaniel W. Faxon (ed.), *The Hospital in Contemporary Life,* Cambridge, Mass., 1949.

[13] *A Pattern for Hospital Care,* Chapters 6, 7.

[14] Klarman, *Hospital Care in New York City.*

philanthropy contributed an average of 4.3 per cent; in the seven midwest and far west cities, it averaged 2.8 per cent.

Equally striking were the variations that were found to exist within each region. In one city on the east coast the philanthropic contribution was as low as 1.7 per cent, with two others just one-tenth of a per cent higher; at the upper extreme, one city had a ratio of 7.2 per cent, followed by two others at 4.5 and 3.6 per cent. In the midwest and far west, the city with the highest ratio of philanthropic funds to total income reached the 4.9 mark, followed by those with 3.7 and 3.4 per cent. The lowest contribution ratio of all cities surveyed was in this region; there, philanthropy represented only 1.3 per cent of total income.[15]

Klarman went on to investigate whether, as appeared likely, the proportion of philanthropic funds was inversely correlated with the proportion of tax funds to total income. But this was not the case, and he concluded that the key to an understanding of regional and local differences had to be sought in history and tradition.[16]

Klarman's detailed analysis of philanthropy's role in the financing of hospital care in New York City disclosed a most interesting fact about the components of the philanthropic contribution that had previously escaped notice. Between 1934 and 1948 centrally raised contributions (United Hospital Fund and Greater New York Fund) increased rapidly—from about $1.5 to $6.4 million annually; other contributions (mostly cash) increased from about $3.0 to $4.8 million. During these fourteen years there was no change in income from total investments which remained at $3.6 million. However, in the period 1948 to 1957 there was only a modest increase in centrally raised funds (from $6.4 to $8.0 million), a relatively larger increase in other contributions ($4.8 to $6.6 million), but a startling advance in income from investments (from $3.6 to $11.2 million).[17]

With few exceptions hospitals outside of New York City and other large eastern centers must rely on current contributions since they do not have endowments. The last two decades have seen, however, a marked trend toward reliance on centrally raised funds for the support of all major philanthropic institutions within the community. In many localities, hospitals participate in these joint campaigns; in others, they do not.

In 1960 the total sums raised in these community campaigns

15 Cf. footnote 6.

16 Klarman, *Hospital Care in New York City.*

17 *Ibid.*

amounted to $458 million—a gain of more than 400 per cent since the outbreak of World War II. Apart from the $57 million allocated to the Red Cross the three largest recipients of the 1960 distribution were recreation, which received $133 million; the support of dependents and social adjustment, which received $115 million; and health, for which $71 million were allocated. But health covered much more than hospitals and clinics; it included the sums distributed to the five major health appeals, outpatient psychiatric clinics, nursing services, and education and research for health agencies. A total of $194 million was raised in 118 cities (each of which raised $500,000 or over). Hospitals, clinics (except psychiatric clinics), and rehabilitation programs received 12.8 per cent of this sum while all health services accounted for 24.8 per cent of the total. Central fund-raising agencies in these larger communities allocated to hospitals a sum of not more than $25 million, and probably somewhat less. This must be put against the total philanthropic income of general hospitals of $200 million, as mentioned earlier.

A few trend data are worth noting. Between 1950 and 1960 total moneys raised by these central fund-raising efforts increased from $193 to $458 million or by about 137 per cent. During this same period total allocations for health increased from $26 to $71 million, or by about 170 per cent. The share received by hospitals and clinics increased by 110 per cent. This indicates that local leadership did not believe that hospitals had special claim to a larger share of the philanthropic dollar; in fact, over the decade they received a somewhat smaller share.[18]

Philanthropy and Capital Funds

The analysis so far has focused on the role of philanthropy in relation to the total operating income of voluntary hospitals. There are several reasons for considering also, at least briefly, the part played by philanthropy in meeting the capital needs of voluntary hospitals. The sums provided by philanthropy for this purpose have been and continue to be substantial.

Between 1950 and 1958 the assets of all of our short-term voluntary hospitals increased from approximately $3.3 billion to $7.2 billion. Total operating expenses of these hospitals, exclusive of the costs of

[18] *1960 Allocations,* United Community Funds and Councils of America, Bulletin No. 211.

new construction, amounted to $1.5 billion in 1950 and $3.5 billion in 1958.[19] The juxtaposition of these capital and operating figures underscores the importance of including capital requirements and resources in any review of the hospital situation. Their intimate relation is also manifested by the fact that three years of operating costs of a bed equals or exceeds the cost of new construction; this emphasizes the potential financial dangers inherent in excess capacity. Depreciation, which amounts to at least 6 per cent of operating expenditures, may or may not be included in current costs, depending on how the hospital prefers to secure funds for renovation and expansion. The period since World War II has been characterized by a shortage of general hospital beds in most regions. This is a result of such factors as limited construction during the 1930's and World War II, the steady rise and dispersion of the population, and the increasing use of hospital facilities. This shortage led to the passage of the Hill-Burton Act in 1946 which made federal funds available (if matched by other levels of government and private funds) for the construction of public and nonprofit hospitals and health centers and related facilities.

A survey report as of December 31, 1960, disclosed that 5,390 projects costing $4.67 billion were aided through this Act, of which $1.45 billion was the federal share. General hospital projects received about four-fifths of all federal funds expended and accounted for about an equal percentage of all new beds. Fifty-five per cent of all the inpatient beds were added in nonprofit institutions which received just about the same percentage of the total moneys made available by the federal government. During the past few years there have been several interesting shifts in the program in favor of grants to institutions desiring to make additions and alterations. Further, more of the projects approved for support have been in nonprofit institutions and more of the federal funds have been allocated to them, so that their share has now reached about three-fifths of the total.[20]

Klarman is responsible for the only careful estimate of the distribution of expenditures for construction by source of funds. His data cover the decade 1948–57, during which he estimates that approximately $8.5 billion was spent on hospital construction. Of this sum, private sources, primarily income from philanthropy but also including mortgages, loans, etc., accounted for 42 per cent of the total, or slightly over $3.5 billion. The federal government contributed ap-

[19] *Statistical Abstract of the United States,* 1960, p. 78.

[20] *Hill-Burton Program, Progress Report,* December 31, 1960, U.S. Department of Health, Education, and Welfare.

proximately 20 per cent and the remaining 38 per cent was made available by state and local government.[21]

In a brochure issued in 1961 by the American Association of Fund-Raising Counsel, it is estimated that in the last twenty-five years philanthropic support for new construction of nonprofit hospitals totaled about $2.6 billion, in contrast to $1.8 billion of charitable contributions for current operations. In addition, nonprofit hospitals received about $500 million in the form of bequests; thus, these hospitals received a grand total of almost $4.9 billion during these years.[22]

These data substantiate Klarman's findings that the larger share of philanthropy's effort with respect to voluntary hospitals has been devoted to the financing of construction and renovation, not to meeting operating costs; in the 1950's, an average annual contribution of under $200 million for current operations was made in contrast to approximately $350 million for capital purposes.

It is worth noting that according to Klarman's data, philanthropy in New York City contributed a greater proportion than in any other large city toward the operating expenses of voluntary hospitals, but provided a smaller share than average for capital purposes. The proportion during the 1950's was 35 per cent; in the rest of the country it was 42 per cent.

Some sense of the magnitude of the postwar construction cycle can be gained by considering developments in New York City. The Hospital Council of Greater New York estimated that about one-third of all voluntary hospital beds today resulted from postwar construction. About half of the large municipal hospital plant is new, and about 30 per cent of the beds in proprietary hospitals came from building which was started after 1945. In the ten hospitals which are supported by the Federation of Jewish Philanthropies, $70 million of new construction was undertaken after the war, and approximately two-thirds of all the beds in the Federation system are new.[23]

While the bulk of capital funds made available to voluntary hospitals is used for new construction, expansion, or renovation of beds for inpatients, attention should be called to one other major purpose for which capital funds have recently been allocated—medical research. The past decade has witnessed a very rapid expansion of medical research. In 1950 total expenditures for this purpose approximated $150 million, while in 1960 they came to $715 million. The federal

[21] Klarman, *Hospital Care in New York City*.

[22] *Giving USA*, 1961 edition, pp. 20 ff.

[23] Ginzberg and Rogatz, *Planning for Better Hospital Care*, Chapter VII.

government has taken the initiative in setting the pace, largely through the instrumentality of the National Institutes of Health, and in 1960 it contributed $425 of the $715 million national total.[24]

Industry and philanthropy, as well as state and local governments, have also increased their contributions to research during recent years. The 1961 edition of *Giving USA* estimates that philanthropy contributes about $90 million a year to medical research. The complex financial relations which exist between universities, medical schools, and the major teaching hospitals preclude any refined estimates of the full impact of these trends on the financing of medical research in voluntary hospitals. But a few points should be noted. A voluntary hospital that wants to remain in the vanguard must create and maintain a good research and teaching environment. While it can look to government, as well as to industry and the foundations, for most of the operating funds required and even for some construction moneys, it must also seek financing for some of the overhead required to enter into and sustain sound programs in postgraduate training and research. Here is a new and what may be an increasing demand for philanthropic support.

Trends in Medical and Hospital Financing

In 1929 aggregate expenditures for health and medical care totaled approximately $3.6 billion. By 1959 the total had risen to $25 billion. In the intervening years, however, population had increased rapidly and the price structure was inflated so that the increase in real per capita terms was less than threefold. In 1959 the per capita expenditures amounted to $142, compared with about $50 in 1929.

In 1935, the total outlay in current prices for health and medical care amounted to $3.26 billion. Private expenditures (including about 2.5 per cent from philanthropy) accounted for 79 per cent of total health and medical expenditures; of the remaining 21 per cent, approximately 17 per cent were state and local and 4 per cent federal. In 1959 when total outlays had risen to above $25 billion, private expenditures had declined to about 75 per cent; there was no significant change in the philanthropic contribution which remained at around 2.5 per cent. On the governmental side, state and local expenditures declined to about 15 per cent and federal expenditures in-

[24] *Coordination of Federal Agencies' Programs in Biomedical Research and in Other Scientific Areas,* 87th Congress, 1st session, Senate Report No. 142, March 30, 1961.

creased to just under 10 per cent, reflecting in the first instance increased hospital expenditures for the military and veterans and a tremendous acceleration of effort in behalf of medical research.[25]

These trend data can be summarized thus: in the quarter century between 1935 and 1959 total expenditures for health and medical care advanced very rapidly, almost threefold on a per capita basis after eliminating the inflationary factor. Consumer expenditures accounted for most of this increase, although there had been a modest increase in the governmental share of from 21 to 25 per cent of the total. The relative proportion of philanthropy had not changed significantly from the beginning to the end of this period.

During this period, the outlay for short-term nonfederal hospitalization increased substantially both absolutely and relatively; it accounted for about one-fifth of the total in 1959 compared to one-seventh twenty-five years earlier. At the same time, the philanthropic contribution to the operating income of short-term nonfederal hospitals declined from almost one-seventh to one-twenty-fifth.

A major revolution occurred in the financing of general hospital care, mostly in the period after World War II. At the center of the revolution was the expansion of hospital and medical insurance. In 1948 private expenditures for hospital services, including outpatient services, totaled about $1.7 billion, of which about one quarter was met by insurance. In 1959, the corresponding figures were over $5 billion and 53 per cent. The prepayment mechanism for hospital expenditures undoubtedly made possible the vastly increased income of hospitals during this period, and further contributed to the corresponding declines in the share of government and philanthropy in the financing of short-term hospital care.[26]

Issues in Hospital Financing

An effort will be made in this section to identify some of the more important policy issues that underlie the structure of hospital financing, with particular reference to the role of philanthropy, and to suggest some of the implications of alternative solutions.

Assuming a continued high level of employment and output, there is no reason to question the ability of the American public to pay for short-term hospital care primarily through the mechanism of

[25] *Ibid.*

[26] Agnes W. Brewster, "Voluntary Health Insurance and Private Medical Care Expenditures, 1948–49," in *Social Security Bulletin,* December, 1960.

insurance, even if the cost of such care continues to rise rapidly as it undoubtedly will. But a problem does exist with respect to the financing of hospital care for those members of the community who cannot pay insurance premiums because they do not have sufficient income and for those who, because they represent adverse risks (age), cannot obtain insurance under existing plans. It is clearly necessary for government to cover the costs of hospitalization for those who are not insured and who have no resources, especially since the sums made available by philanthropy to nonprofit short-term hospitals are inadequate.

In the past government became responsible for many patients who initially were able to pay for their hospitalization either directly or through insurance but who exhausted their savings or their benefits during the course of a prolonged illness. To reduce the incidence of such indigency, government, together with voluntary leadership in the health field, should strive constantly to secure an improvement in the quality of insurance benefits. For relatively small additions in premiums, it is possible to increase substantially the number of days of coverage. Recent developments in the field of catastrophic medical insurance are a further step in the direction of providing the type of protection that is required.

More difficult is the problem that faces older persons who are not currently enrolled in a hospital insurance program, who are unable to maintain their membership, or who are not permitted to convert their group membership to an individual policy when they leave employment and are forced out of a group plan. Here, too, progress is being made, for many group plans now provide for conversion to individual coverage after retirement. And state governments are constantly restricting the freedom of profit and nonprofit carriers to deny individuals the opportunity for such conversion.

The current agitation in favor of including hospital benefits for individuals over sixty-five under the Social Security system reflects a response to the serious lack of coverage at the present time for many older persons. However, without blanketing in the large numbers who are currently outside of the Social Security system the passage of one of the pending proposals will not solve the problem for the substantial proportion of the older group which is uncovered at present. It would of course insure coverage for all those who are now in the system as well as those who may later be added.

The issue can be formulated thus: is it necessary or desirable to modify the present Social Security system in this major regard or will the evolutionary changes in insurance practices currently under way provide a satisfactory alternative for most people who have not yet reached sixty-five years of age? To what extent should the public assistance mechanism continue to be relied upon and to what extent should use be made of the generally preferred mechanism of Social Security? To what extent is easier access to general hospitals crucial for meeting the health needs of older persons?

It should be recognized that payment for hospitalization is not the main problem from the viewpoint of the individual patient though it is of central concern to the hospital. The patient is concerned with the total costs that he must meet—before he enters the hospital, while an inpatient, and after he has been discharged. These costs involve fees to the physician and other essential expenditures. While hospitalization may cost the patient $40 a day, round-the-clock nursing, if he requires it, will come to almost $60 a day more; and the fees of the physician who treats him in the hospital may equal or exceed his total hospital bill. For this reason prepayment plans have expanded rapidly in recent years to cover part or all of the fees that the patient must pay to the physician while in the hospital. Little progress has been made, however, with prepayment for nursing services, except under catastrophic insurance. Since 1948 the proportion of all expenditures for services in and out of the hospital covered by insurance increased from 6 to 29 per cent. In 1959, these expenditures came within 10 per cent of total private outlays for hospital services.[27] The combined premiums for hospital and physicians' services in the hospital, however, have been advancing rapidly and an important question is the extent to which those in the lower income groups can afford to meet them. The rising public clamor in many communities where Blue Cross has recently advanced its rates substantially is indicative of mounting consumer annoyance, if not resistance. It is questionable whether, without substantial employer participation in the payment of such premiums, many at the lower end of the income scale will be able to afford these mounting premiums. Here is a major threat to hospital financing.

The rapidly mounting premiums make it desirable to consider whether any factors now included in hospital charges could properly be excluded so as to enhance the ability of persons with low incomes to participate or continue to participate in prepayment plans. It was noted earlier that substantial educational and, to a lesser degree, research costs are currently included in hospital cost and charge struc-

[27] *Ibid.*

tures. Their deletion, however, would probably not permit a reduction of more than 5 or 10 per cent in the charges levied by hospitals with comprehensive teaching and research programs. Such relief would not be sufficient to affect the mounting disparity between hospital costs and the consumer's disposable income, especially for those who are at the lower end of the income distribution. Between 1950 and 1957 the percentage of disposable income spent for hospital care increased by almost one-third.[28] There are good reasons to rationalize the support of postgraduate medical teaching and research even if it will not do more than make a minor contribution to the specific problem at hand—to help assure the financial solvency of a broadly based prepayment plan. Unless the community rationalizes these costs many hospitals will not be able to establish the range and quality of educational programs that are required to provide the necessary numbers of well-trained medical personnel. Among the many blocks to expanding the number of physicians are the formidable costs involved in operating good teaching hospitals.

There is a clear and urgent need to strengthen the modest controls that are currently exercised by government and voluntary organizations in determining the number and type of hospital beds that a community or an area requires. It is generally acknowledged that the Hill-Burton Act encouraged the construction of too many small hospitals to permit effective staffing. From the viewpoint of controlling costs no action promises more return than sound policies directed toward preventing the unnecessary expansion of hospital facilities or the duplication of expensive services. Excess hospital beds and duplication of specialized services are not only a sure way to waste capital funds but they further insure unnecessarily high operating costs. Hospitals with empty beds are likely to keep patients longer than is medically indicated—especially if their physicians know that insurance will cover their patients' bills.

There is no easy answer as to how more effective controls can be assured. At a minimum, state governments should consider issuing charters to new hospitals only on the basis of certificates of necessity, and they might well consider exercising similar controls over large-scale expansion programs of established hospitals. Most important, all units of government—federal, state, and local—which play such a large role in making funds available for new construction, should restudy and tighten the criteria governing the allocation and use of

[28] Ginzberg and Rogatz, *Planning for Better Hospital Care,* p. 69.

these funds. Similarly, various voluntary groups that are directly or indirectly involved in raising substantial sums for the capital or operating needs of voluntary hospitals should insist upon adequate planning studies as background for their allocations.[29] Rugged individualism in hospital operations is an anachronism.[30]

Among the less desirable consequences of the vast expansion of hospital insurance has been its impact on the manner in which scarce medical resources are used. While the key to such utilization remains the physician and the manner in which he practices his profession, hospital insurance has contributed to the underutilization of specialized hospital resources by limiting insurance benefits primarily to inpatients. This tends to raise hospital costs and insurance premiums. From the community's point of view it would be much more desirable to have the hospital's specialized facilities used by both in- and outpatients. Since room and board loom large in total hospital costs the costs of treating ambulatory patients can be kept much below those for inpatients.

Another axis along which progress can be made is to insure a higher level of planning among the major interest groups—hospitals, government, and insurance systems. Instances have come to light in the last few years where the interlocking directorships of Blue Cross and voluntary hospitals resulted in the absence of countervailing pressures to assure that resources in a noncompetitive market are well allocated and used. Only danger and eventually insolvency for both the voluntary hospital and the prepayment plans can result if the hospital continues to expect Blue Cross to reimburse it on the basis of average costs. To avoid this, the hospital must exercise restraint over policies which tend to raise costs. Moreover, a prepayment plan that acts as nothing more than a conduit for funds which pass from the consumer to the producer has a limited future.

The hospital is a unique institution in that no one person or group of persons has clear cut responsibility for its management. Legally the board of trustees has this responsibility but in fact the trustees have remarkably little influence on the way in which the staff, particularly the medical staff, functions. While it is obviously sensible to leave the treatment of patients to the physician, it should be recognized that

[29] Hospital Planning Association of Allegheny County, *Executive Director's Report,* May 23, 1960.

[30] Eli Ginzberg, "The Hospital and the Community," in *The Impact of the Antibiotics on Medicine and Society,* Iago Galdston, ed., New York, 1958.

much of what occurs in the hospital relates more to the convenience of the physician than to the needs of the patient.

The hospital is unique also in that its resources, provided in part by community funds, are essential for the conduct of private medical practice. Years ago it was argued that the physician gave so much free service in caring for charity patients that he returned to the community much more than he received. It is questionable whether a careful application of a cost-benefit calculus would ever have supported this conclusion. It is even more doubtful in recent years which have witnessed a steady decline in the proportion of charity patients.

The basic question, however, is what can be done to establish effective centers of authority and responsibility within each voluntary hospital so that a continuing effort can be made to use the resources of these multimillion dollar institutions efficiently. The answer must be found by those who provide the operating and capital resources. They are the parties of major interest; they are the ones who must devote interest and imagination to this question.

No student of medical economics believes that the trend towards rising hospital costs can be reversed. But the wide range of controls that have been identified above and the many more that might be identified suggest that much can be done to slow the rate of advance, if the community is sufficiently interested and concerned. There is some evidence that the significant gains made since World War II to underpin and strengthen the financing of general hospital care will be jeopardized unless community efforts are accelerated and intensified. The community has a further interest in seeing to it that only hospitals that meet certain minimum standards have the opportunity to participate in governmental grant and nonprofit reimbursement programs.[31]

Comparisons with Education

The preceding analysis of the changing role of philanthropy in the financing of short-term hospital care in nonfederal hospitals has delineated the following major trends. The relative significance of philanthropy as a source of general hospital operating income has declined precipitously during the last three decades. The relative share of the government's contribution has also declined. It is the consumer's share, directly and through insurance, which has substantially increased.

[31] Harold M. and Anne R. Somers, *Doctors, Patients and Health Insurance,* Washington, D.C., 1961, passim.

With regard to capital resources the trend has been notably different. Before World War II philanthropy was the primary source of funds for the construction of hospitals providing short-term care. While philanthropy has continued to contribute sizeable sums for capital purposes the most significant postwar development has been the increasing role of government—federal, state, and local—in providing capital funds. To complete the picture reference must be made to the vastly enlarged role of the federal government in providing general hospital care for the large number of men and women on active military duty as well as for the significant number of veterans. In 1935, the total medical and hospital care expenditures for the military and veteran groups amounted to well under $100 million; in 1959 the corresponding figure was in excess of $1 billion.

Some gain in perspective may be achieved by considering recent developments in the financing of education. For education, like hospital and medical care, also depends on mixed financing from government, private, and philanthropic funds. In 1930, of the approximately $2.6 billion of total combined operating and capital expenditures for elementary and secondary education, private funds accounted for $235 million, or 9 per cent. By 1950, when the total had risen to $6.7 billion, private expenditures amounted to $790 million, almost 12 per cent. The comparable data for 1958 are $15.0 billion total, of which $2.1 were private funds; that is, the private sector had risen to 14 per cent of the total. These figures reveal that public expenditures had risen about five and one-half times during these three decades, but private expenditures had increased by almost tenfold.

Expenditures for higher education underwent an even more rapid expansion, from $630 million in 1930 to almost $4.7 billion in 1958. While private expenditures exceeded public expenditures for the fifteen years preceding 1945, the trend shifted after World War II; in 1958 public funds accounted for roughly 60 per cent of the total.[32]

It is not feasible to develop a reliable estimate of the role of philanthropy in the support of private elementary and secondary education but a few observations may be helpful. About five of the seven million pupils in private schools are enrolled in Catholic schools which rely substantially on members of religious orders for staff. Moreover, Catholics also raise substantial funds for capital purposes. It is further general knowledge that parochial schools adjust their fees or waive them in the case of able young people from poor homes.

The larger independent secondary schools have an estimated en-

[32] *Health, Education, and Welfare Trends,* 1960 edition, U.S. Department of Health, Education, and Welfare.

dowment of about $200 million and the 101 that reported to the American Alumni Council in 1959–60 had total gift income of about $23 million.[33]

Philanthropy has always played a more important role in financing higher than elementary or secondary education. In 1930, the philanthropic share of the total income of institutions of higher learning amounted to 17 per cent; government contributed 31 per cent, student fees accounted for 26 per cent, and income from sales and from auxiliary enterprises accounted for the remainder. These ratios were not significantly affected by the major depression but they were radically altered after World War II. In 1958 philanthropic income, though it had risen from under $100 million in 1930 to over $500 million, declined from 17 to 11 per cent of the total income. The governmental share had increased from 31 to 43 per cent. Student fees had actually declined from 26 to 20 per cent.[34]

From these selective figures it is clear that the pattern of financing education differs markedly from that of general hospitals. In brief, at each level of the educational system, government has always played a larger role than in the financing of general hospital care. In higher education in which the private and the public sectors were more nearly matched than in elementary and secondary education, governmentally supported institutions have grown more rapidly in recent years than private institutions. The consumer's share of total expenditures for elementary and secondary education has increased but today he is actually covering a smaller proportion of the total sum spent for higher education than he did in 1930. Philanthropy has increased its contributions to higher education substantially for both capital and operating purposes but it provides today only $1 out of every $9 of current income. This, however, compares very favorably with its contributions to nonprofit hospitals, where it provides only about $1 in $25.

There are, however, a few parallels between the two fields that should be noted. Various levels of government have enabled private institutions of higher learning, mostly through loans, to expand their facilities. To date the sums made available fall short of the level of support provided through the Hill-Burton Act but they are nonetheless significant. There has been some interesting experimentation in the postpayment of educational expenditures through the establishment of various systems of student loans. Various banks and insurance companies have developed college savings programs that aim at pre-

[33] *Giving USA,* 1961 edition, pp. 12 ff.

[34] *Health, Education and Welfare Trends.*

accumulation, at least a distant reminder of Blue Cross's prepayment principle.

Many universities are benefiting from large research and special teaching grants made by government, and to a lesser degree the stronger teaching hospitals are also able to draw on this kind of support. Finally various governmental programs which make grants to individuals enable many to cover the high costs of education or medical care.

Broader Perspectives

A detailed consideration of the changing pattern of the financing of general hospital care, which today is a $5 billion industry, should provide a delineation of some important facets of our changing economy and society. In this concluding section an effort will be made to identify briefly some of those broad implications.

1. Philanthropy has never been able adequately to pay for the products or services required by any substantial segment of the population. Its ability to compensate for skewness in the income distribution has always been limited.

2. In an economy characterized by rapid increases in per capita real income and in disposable income there is no reason for the community to place heavy reliance on philanthropy to provide funds for the production of basic services.

3. In periods of rapid expansion in the demand for services traditionally provided by institutions that derive important support from philanthropy, it has not been possible for philanthropy to maintain its proportionate share of the total income, particularly if the enhanced demand coincides with a period of price inflation.

4. In times of increased demand and inflated prices, there is a serious danger that institutions that have long relied on philanthropy for a significant portion of their total income will be unable to compete successfully for scarce resources, particularly trained personnel, because of the traditional lag in adjusting charges to current costs. As a result of this lag they significantly underpay their staffs, jeopardize future recruitment, and are forced to provide an inferior quality of service.

5. This weakened economic position of many hospitals is likely to be reflected in underinvestment in plant and equipment with serious consequences for the efficiency with which scarce resources are employed and social objectives are met.

6. The substantial changes in the level of national income and in the distribution of personal income over the past several decades, and the likelihood of further changes in the decades ahead, underscore the importance of potentially radical innovations in the financing of essential services. Such innovations occurred in hospital care during the 1950's and are now under way in higher education.

7. As long as the cold war continues it is questionable whether government alone, regardless of the pattern of federal-state-local fiscal relations, can devote adequate funds to insure services of appropriate quantity and quality for the education, health, and welfare of the public. The country has backed into mixed patterns of financing in many of these fields. It is a major challenge to evaluate existing designs critically in order to improve upon them. By so doing, the sums that consumers can contribute towards the purchase of such services may be enlarged and appropriate levels of capital investment in human resources and facilities may be assured.

8. Philanthropic institutions have long presented a serious challenge from the viewpoint of efficient management. They have been the preferred environments for amateurism, nepotism, and narrow group interests. Now that many of these institutions have become large-scale enterprises there is an urgent need, if valuable resources are not to be poorly utilized and wasted, to improve their management. The fact that it will not be easy is no excuse to back away from the challenge.

9. The best way to improve the internal management of these institutions is through community, regional, and national planning. Here the incentive must come from those who make the funds available, for they are the ones primarily concerned to see that their money goes as far as possible.

10. Finally, economists and other social scientists have a responsibility to develop studies that will lead to the emergence of sounder criteria than now exist to guide investment and pricing policy. Such studies will have to be more than exercises in geometry or calculus for the core values of a democratic society impinge directly on the education, health, and welfare of the public and these are not reducible to mathematical terms. Economists have special capabilities in analyzing problems in the allocation of scarce resources. Until recently the leaders of the profession have been deeply interested in welfare. A renewed interest in welfare problems can result not only in substantial social benefit but will also help to revitalize an academic tradition that is in danger of becoming irrelevant.

Philanthropy and the Business Corporation, Existing Guidelines—Future Policy

COVINGTON HARDEE
Clark, Carr & Ellis

PHILANTHROPY may exist in many forms, as the work of the National Bureau of Economic Research and of this conference amply demonstrates. Historically, philanthropy begins with the individual acting privately and under the compulsion of a variety of drives—some of which may appear to contain more altruism than others. A later development is the institutionalization of aid by means of the private foundation which the law recognizes as an entity separate from its creator. The foundation may be simple or highly organized as the circumstances and the donor's wishes determine; it may take the form of a trust or of a nonprofit corporation. Traditionally foundations have been employed where large amounts of capital are to be devoted to charitable purposes and where the donor intends that the income from invested capital or, in the case of self-liquidating foundations, income and part principal over a period of years, be used to carry out his philanthropic aims. More recently philanthropic individuals have come to realize that the private foundation offers tax and other advantages for even the small donor.

The charitable foundation is a unique creation of private enterprise capitalism in the United States. The encouragement which our polity has given to the creation and development of this institution, through tax incentives, has resulted in the accumulation of significant amounts of capital devoted to bettering the conditions of human life in our society. The significance and substantiality of this wholly private, nongovernmental activity is little understood outside the North Atlantic capitalist community. If more time and effort were spent in informing alien cultures of the connection between private enterprise capitalism and the philanthropic activities carried on by U.S. private foundations abroad, a more favorable image of our social system could be developed.

Some students, such as Frank Dickinson, consider that another form of philanthropy is public philanthropy. Just which governmental activities should be so classified is to some extent an exercise in semantics. It should be remembered that the labels we pin on things affect our thinking about them, and the way we think in turn affects our acts. The notion that governmental activity of any sort may be properly termed "philanthropy" seems to some observers quite erroneous. It is certainly true that the government distributes social benefits which are paid for in most cases by taxpayers other than the recipients. Such benefits, however, are generally distributed pursuant to legislation enacted because the legislators think that the recipients are *entitled* to them. Thus, Social Security benefits, to the extent that they are not paid for by the workers, should be regarded as representing a Congressional decision concerning the *proper* distribution of the fruits of private enterprise. This is certainly not philanthropy in the ordinary usage of that term. It might be better subsumed under the heading of "social justice." Whether one agrees with the propriety of the system or the quantum of the benefits is, of course, beside the point.

Beyond these more or less traditional forms of philanthropy or social welfare we come to the newest type—corporation philanthropy. Like individual philanthropy, it may be conducted by the corporation itself or through a separate legal entity—either a trust or a corporation. The growth of company giving over the past two decades warrants considerable study. We need to examine the why, the wherefore and especially the whither. We need to know what motivates management in directing part of the fruits of private enterprise in this or that direction. We need to know whether the decision-making is good or bad, whether the trend is more or less favorable to the good society, whether these activities should be encouraged or discouraged. The purpose of this paper is to lay the groundwork for a discussion directed to these questions.

It has recently been pointed out that:

> A noisy sector of the legal front is all but quiet. Where the clamor was, was little more, for this small war was less than a battle, and its spoils more

> form than substance. In the name of social need and institutional responsibility, the remnants of greed have been swept aside and the law has proclaimed that the business corporation may love mankind. Indeed, it may express its love in a most practical way—with dollars.[1]

While it is true that litigation involving corporate power to make charitable contributions is rare (indeed, such power has seldom been invalidated in this century), it would be a great mistake to assume that management is free from constraint in such matters. This may be demonstrated by a study of the steps taken by the Union Pacific Railroad Company to insure that its corporate contribution program was placed not only beyond the realm of successful legal attack, but indeed beyond the range of responsible criticism.

In 1953 the Board of Directors of the Union Pacific Railroad Company began to consider the question of putting its contributions program on an expanded basis. Over the years, the Company had been making contributions to organizations which had a close tie-in with railroad operations, such as Travelers' Aid and Red Cross. Corporate power to make such contributions was never questioned and would doubtless be sustained under the common-law test of validity—direct benefit to the corporation. This test was laid down in the 19th century in the famous old case of *Hutton* v. *West Cork Railway,* 23 Ch. Div. 654 (1893). The Board of Union Pacific concluded, however, that in its traditional contributions the Company may not have been fully discharging its responsibility as a corporate citizen. Many felt that Union Pacific could and should do more to strengthen and expand educational, welfare and cultural activity in the areas it serves. To this end, a special committee of the Board was created to give thought to the matter and report to the full Board its recommendations for action.

The report of the Contributions Advisory Committee of the Board was rendered in June 1954. It was supported by counsel's opinion noting the absence of statutory or case law in Utah, the state from which the company derived its corporate powers, concerning corporate power to make charitable contributions. The Committee and counsel jointly suggested a course of action designed to supply the needed legitimacy. This would encompass: first, the preparation and proposal of legislation adding charity to the list of powers possessed by Utah corporations; second, the formation of the Union Pacific Railroad Foundation as a nonprofit corporation under the laws of Utah; third,

1 B. S. Prunty, Jr., "Love and the Business Corporation," *Virginia Law Review,* April 1960, p. 467.

a modest contribution to the Foundation by the Company; fourth, a contribution by the Foundation to an eleemosynary institution; fifth, a test case in the Utah courts establishing the legality of the foregoing under the Utah law.

The preparation of legislation was not difficult since the Company's counsel had available the work of a very fine committee of the American Bar Association, which had prepared a model statute expressly granting to corporations the power to make philanthropic contributions. The strong public-interest flavor of the legislation and its eminent sponsorship made it easy to develop the necessary political support for it. The bill was passed in the 1955 session of the Utah legislature and promptly approved by the Governor. It provided that corporations organized under the laws of Utah "shall have the power . . . to make donations for the public welfare or for charitable, scientific, religious or educational purposes." [2]

The Union Pacific Railroad Foundation was organized May 13, 1955 as a membership corporation under Utah law; that is, instead of stockholders, the corporation has members. No stock is ever issued. The membership is a self-perpetuating body, vacancies being filled by the remaining members. The duty of the membership is to elect annually a Board of Trustees, who in turn decide on policy and select the executive officers. The membership of the Union Pacific Railroad Foundation is restricted by its charter to persons who are also directors of the Union Pacific Railroad Company. The trustees of the Foundation are in practice Board members of the Union Pacific Railroad Company or its subsidiaries. Provisions in the charter for electing a minority of outside or public trustees have never been exercised.

When organization was complete, the test contributions were made; $5,000 by the Company to the Foundation and $4,000 by the Foundation to Brigham Young University, an institution operated by the Church of Jesus Christ of Latter Day Saints. The latter gift was earmarked one-half to current income and one-half to capital requirements of the university. The stage was thus set for the litigation testing the validity of the Company's actions. The gifts were made with the provision that, if judicially invalidated, they were required to be returned.

The test litigation which ensued was patterned on the well-known case of *A. P. Smith Co.* v. *Barlow,* which established the validity of charitable contributions by corporations organized under the laws of

[2] Utah Code Annotated (1953), Ch. 16-2-14(8).

New Jersey. That case held that a gift by a company to Princeton University was valid under the recently passed New Jersey statute and would have been valid even without statutory sanction by reason of judicial expansion of the notion of what constitutes "benefit" to the corporation—the traditional requirement of the common law deriving from the *Hutton* case referred to above.

To set the stage for the litigation it was necessary to find some stockholder members of what might be called a loyal opposition. Stockholders were found who were willing to write to the company stating their opposition to the Company's program under the existing Utah law. Thereupon, the Company commenced action against the complaining stockholders, requesting the Utah courts to declare that the Company's activities were valid under the Utah statute and would have been valid even if the statute had not been enacted. Depositions were taken from various Union Pacific directors as to the reasons for the Board's action. John Watson of the National Industrial Conference Board testified to the growth and importance of corporate philanthropy in the United States. The trial court decided that the Company had acted improperly, that Utah corporations lacked power under the common law to make gifts to charity and that the statute could not apply to a corporation organized prior to its effective date.

Nothing daunted by this unfavorable, and somewhat irrational, decision, the Company's attorneys appealed. They informed the management that the result in the trial court merely confirmed the advisability of proceeding with utmost caution. Fortunately, the Supreme Court of Utah reversed the trial court. The decision on appeal, though gratifying as to result, was unsatisfactory in its reasoning. Union Pacific's activities were upheld under the common law, but the Court refused to pass on the applicability of the statute, on the grounds that the statute itself made no mention of applicability to pre-existing corporations. This omission was remedied in 1961 when a new business corporation law was passed, reenacting the charitable power and making all provisions of the new law applicable to pre-existing corporations.

The time and effort expended by Union Pacific in establishing the legitimacy of its charitable efforts is a graphic illustration, I believe, of the importance management attributes to being above criticism in the touchy area of giving away "other people's money." Fear of an attack based on *ultra vires* (exceeding authorized powers) is not the only constraint upon management's judgment. The outer limits on the quantum of giving are controlled by statute in some states and, as a practical matter, by the federal income tax laws, which limit to 5 per cent of taxable income the amount of charitable giving which is deductible for tax purposes.

The acts of directors of corporations are controlled in another important way as well. Directors are required to exercise reasonable business judgment in all of their decisions. Existence of a corporate power to make contributions is not license to give any amount to any donee. An undefined perimeter exists, measured by what seems reasonable under the circumstances (reasonableness being determined by the courts upon shareholder challenge). Directors exceeding these bounds do so at peril of being held liable for wasting company assets. This is an effective sanction even though no recent cases have been found where directors have been held liable for straying beyond the permitted territory. Indeed, since litigation itself is expensive and involves unfavorable publicity, the existence of the barrier tends to make management lean over backward to be safe from attack. We cannot, therefore, expect company-sponsored foundations to engage in the kind of experimental programming and subsidization of work on the frontiers of sociology, which are and must remain the prized preserve of private foundations in our pluralistic order.

The fact that certain boundaries and limitations on managerial discretion exist does not mean that we should be complacent about the developing role of company-sponsored foundations. The funds devoted to these purposes are bound to grow as more and more companies join in corporate philanthropy and as the unexpended capital increases. We should, therefore, direct our attention to the question: what can be done to improve the usefulness of these entities to our society? One suggestion will be advanced here; it is hoped that others may be developed in colloquy.

The encouragement of professionalism in management is a phenomenon of twentieth century capitalism. That same attitude, which is responsible for the wide acceptance of business schools, conference boards, management associations, and company-sponsored executive training programs, should be applied to corporate philanthropy. Far from deriding the "philanthropoid," companies should welcome the role of the professional giver. Private foundations, the training ground for professionalism in philanthropy, should expect and indeed look forward to some raiding of their ranks for the importation of trained personnel into company-sponsored foundations. To some extent this has already begun, but it must be encouraged and increased.

The fact that company-sponsored foundations must pursue a more cautious course than private foundations is no excuse for turning over their funds, as is sometimes done, to the company public-relations department. The company foundation should be thought of as tied to the company's objectives but with some degree of independence in reaching them. It should have a fully developed and trained staff without other company duties or responsibilities. Existing means for exchanging views between companies and for developing sound philanthropic policy should be strengthened. Exchange of views should not be limited to such questions as respective opinions of the *X* charitable organization, or whether to support a particular appeal.

Where the company foundation is too small to permit the development of its own professional staff, outside help should be sought. Already there exist men of national repute in the field, whose services are available on a consultative basis. Sound policy-making and programming is available to even small company-sponsored foundations through this means. Attendance at various meetings and conferences on corporate philanthropy, such as those conducted from time to time by the National Industrial Conference Board and biennially by New York University, is another way for the small-company foundation to participate in the development of sound objectives and attitudes for corporate philanthropy.

As professionalism increases and becomes more accepted, we may even look forward to the development of case-method teaching materials in this area. The introduction of courses in college departments of sociology and in the business schools would be of great assistance in attracting the talent and ability of young intellectuals and thus creating a professional cadre for this important work.

Those who believe in having numerous power centers in our society will welcome the growth of institutionalized philanthropy. The sound development of these private entities acts as a counterweight to the growth and importance of the welfare activities of the state. Private enterprise capitalism should therefore lend all support to the growing trend towards professionalism in private philanthropic activity.

The charitable foundation, whether sponsored by an individual or by a company, is an American institution of great and growing importance. This product of the capitalist society, which distributes some of the rewards of capital to cultural and humanitarian activities, is a tangible result of the realization by property owners and managers of duties and responsibilities over and above those imposed by law. It is likewise a refutation of the dogma that American culture is purely materialistic. The new awakening, whether motivated by love of man or fear of the consequences of non-action, is a powerful force for good in our order. It remains for us to make certain that the new image of enlightened capitalism is carried to the rest of the world, presently struggling with the outmoded concept of capitalism as a rapacious, dog-eat-dog system with values measured purely by self-interest.

Highlights of the Conference

FRANK G. DICKINSON
National Bureau of Economic Research and Northern Illinois University

THE following brief summary of what was said at the conference is not intended to be a short essay on philanthropy. Rather it contains some of the points and questions which one conferee ranks as the highlights of the conference.

It should be noted that no verbatim record was made of the more than forty-five hours of discussions in the eighteen sessions of the conference. Nor did the Chairman request the participants to furnish citations or data to support their comments. Probably the conferees could have documented their statements, but this would not have been feasible in a discussion-type conference. The conferees were requested to, and many did, suggest changes in a longer preliminary draft, but this short digest stands as an incomplete record of what was said at the conference based largely on one person's impressions. Hence it should be considered similar to the contributed (signed) papers; one person determined which ideas and opinions of the thirty-one conferees should be summarized. This digest, as well as the contributed papers, do not necessarily present the views of the National Bureau or the Merrill Center for Economics, or of a majority of the conferees.

The Boundaries of Philanthropy

At the first session an attempt was made, of course, to circumscribe the area of philanthropy. As Boulding and Vickrey pointed out in their papers, the basic idea of philanthropy seems to exclude the application of a conventional theory of value and of what is known of ordinary market behavior. For philanthropy involves a one-sided exchange; that is, there is no *quid pro quo* unless it is extremely remote.

The conference expressed a hope that confusion could be avoided between the ends served by philanthropy and the methods and procedures used to finance it. Accordingly, an attempt was made to attribute the distinguishing qualifications of philanthropic activity to motivation and voluntarism. But a flurry of examples seemed to indicate that motivation and voluntarism could not be used as a means of circumscribing the content of philanthropy.

In fact, the conference concluded its eighteen sessions without locating the current boundaries of philanthropy. In my opinion, this was one of its virtues because the very opportunity for unbounded discussion of these concepts provided interesting comments on the problems encountered in the attempts of a group to circumscribe a broad and dynamic subject. The inapplicability of the whole mechanism of value theory was clearly recognized again and again by the economists present, and the problem posed thereby in delimiting the subject of philanthropy was well aired.

It was established that the conference should endeavor to discuss philanthropy in the broadest of contexts: not only as a term and as a concept but also as a problem or set of problems in public policy. These are not unrelated. The meeting of new responsibilities by government during the past three decades has wrought a revolution in the manner in which philanthropic goals are achieved. Consequently this conference was left in the throes of some serious definitional dilemmas. Some conferees would apply the term "public philanthropy" to activities of government—foreign or domestic—of a philanthropic character. Other conferees would exclude all forms of public aid from the concept of philanthropy.

The discussion turned from matters of definition to a consideration of the philosophical and historical bases of philanthropic activity. A mere listing of some of the terms suggested as topics for consideration will indicate the scope: philanthropy, charity, benevolence, justice, social justice, religious imperative, religious ethic, status, voluntary and compulsory giving, egalitarianism, public philanthropy, social welfare, social charity, categorical aid in the area of public assistance.

The Future of Philanthropy

Is philanthropy an area where we can expect more nationalization? How much is the future of philanthropy linked to the future expansion of social security? Will higher incomes bring less philanthropy in the future? What will be the trend particularly during the 1960's?

The first speculation was that in the field of health and welfare there would probably be an increasing trend toward nationalization even to the extent of making wealthy as well as poor retired people eligible for free hospital care, and possibly also for some forms of free medical care.

To some conferees the trend of Old Age and Survivors Insurance (OASI) benefits and taxes was not reassuring; they now overshadow public assistance and giving to the traditional areas of private philanthropy. Data were introduced to show that in 1952 probably 96 per cent of the value of the current OASI benefits had not been theoretically prepaid by the retired persons and by their employers; for the current beneficiaries, OASI was 96 per cent Old Age Assistance (OAA). One conferee suggested that social security should be called "philsurance," because the claim that it is insurance has created no small amount of confusion. Most of the conferees did not agree with one who remarked that, if he should live to obtain his social security benefits for himself and for his wife, he would accept only the January check, since that was about as much as he and his employer could have (theoretically) prepaid. He would use the remaining eleven checks each year to transfer the income back to the needy members of the next generation who are being required to provide him with that income.

One of the forces in our democratic society today which will influence the future of philanthropy, it was pointed out, is the increased number of older voters. The proportion of older voters, say those aged 50 and over, will continue to rise until 1970. During the 1960's, therefore, there will be persistent demand for more transfer payments from the young to the old. The market place forces must be taken into account in considering the future of philanthropy. If we were to have a completely insured population or if there were enough corporate pension plans and other provisions for accumulation of savings during the working period of life, the problem of providing assistance in old age would be reduced to a minimum.

The rise in governmental welfare programs may provide an increasing demand for services to be rendered by private organizations but financed by government. Perhaps the chief function of private philanthropy in the future will be to provide capital funds rather than operating funds. Stress was laid on the possibility that, as our people have more leisure time, they will give more time to voluntary agencies.

Public accountability of private philanthropic institutions, it was felt, will continue to be an issue during the 1960's. The number and assets of foundations will increase rapidly, although no conferee gave a specific estimate of growth. A prediction was made that corporate philanthropy would probably increase very rapidly in the 1960's, although much would depend upon the rate of corporate tax. The total support by corporations of philanthropic endeavors, estimated to be almost twice what is reported in corporate income tax returns as "contributions," might reach $2.5 billion a year by 1975.

There was also some speculation about the following: it was agreed that some institutions, such as the county poor house, are disappearing; that hospitals will probably continue to receive a decreasing proportion of income from philanthropy; that such items as playgrounds may be privately financed instead of publicly financed in the future; that government foreign aid, which some do and others do not regard as philanthropy, will increasingly dwarf its ancient counterpart, religious missionary effort, although other private foreign aid may also increase. The discussion of financing the rapid expansion in private and public education yielded no consensus on specific trends. At some future time total expenditures for health could exceed those for education. The prediction of increasing professionalism in philanthropy, especially in private and company-sponsored foundations, was disputed. Finally, several conferees stressed the difficulty of considering the role of philanthropy in a future dominated by missiles and nuclear power involving enormous expenditures.

Private Domestic Philanthropy

Despite the increase in affluence, the expected increases in the income and expenditures of churches are not too evident except for the rapid expansion in provision for religious education. Direct giving of benevolences through churches is one aspect of religious philanthropy; support of the current expenses of the church—the edifice itself, the preaching and teaching responsibilities—is another. The question of income elasticity in relation to this type of giving was discussed briefly, with special reference to Vickrey's paper. Data for 1959 showed that 34 per cent of the charitable bequests in the reported estates under $100,000 was given to religious organizations, but only 6.5 per cent of the bequests of $1 million and over. The larger the bequest, the smaller the proportion given to religious organizations.

In the hospital area, as noted in Ginzberg's paper, one significant trend is that the share of government is going down and private payments for services are increasing; the latter, of course, are not philanthropic. At least one conferee contended that only a minority of Americans still conceives of the hard charity or relief case as being a function of private philanthropy. Those religious groups which continue to stress their responsibility for some special type of philanthropy (such as the care of unsupported children) will probably find in the future that the government will be purchasing more and more of their services.

Foundations

The foundation was by all odds the most popular subject of the eighteen sessions of this conference on philanthropy. Foundations may be classified conveniently into five categories: (1) general research, (2) special purpose, (3) company-sponsored, (4) family or personal, and (5) the community trust or community foundation.

Foundations are among the freest organizations in our economy. They are governed only by their trustees, and there is no substantial government regulation. They do not rely upon contributions and need not defer to contributors. It was contended that foundations can afford to be venturesome (a foundation is not doing a good job unless it derives no value from some of its grants); and that they should provide reasonably full disclosure of their activities at least once annually.

There was considerable discussion about the size of the foundation. It should be large enough, in one view, to expend funds for guidance in the making of grants. But can a foundation be too large? Can the few extremely large foundations—currently there are ten with assets of more than $100 million—exercise an undue influence over foundation giving generally? There is certainly no legal barrier to keep foundations from concentrating research and overbidding for personnel in specific areas. This development, it was held by some conferees, could seriously dislocate some of our universities by bringing too great an increase in the demand for persons working in particular fields of research. Some of the conferees thought that the large foundation had a tendency to pursue academic fads and snowball them, and to concentrate their support on "safe" areas such as medical research. It was pointed out that there is no analogue to the market to enforce discipline upon the foundation. Hence there is a great need within foundations for adequate and competent criticism.

Small foundations, defined by the Foundation Library Center as those with less than $1 million of assets, are increasing at the rate of more than 1,000 a year. A large part of their funds are used to support local and civic projects, including the Girl Scouts and the Boy Scouts, recreation, civic affairs, cultural activities. To some leaders of public opinion this indicates little imagination; to supporters of these activities it is deemed an advantage of the small foundation.

The general research foundations have had a considerable impact on the allocation of trained manpower and resources. They have conceptualized fields of research, exercised leadership, and shown initiative; they have become knowledgeable about the research interests and aspirations of the academic community, and tried to promote them; and they have supported research and developmental projects with large sums. The purpose of a research grant, it was felt, is to encourage the activity rather than to buy the end product of results. Apparently, government support of research is growing rapidly and foundations are becoming relatively less important as a source of research funds in the United States.

Would not these research funds of foundations and government agencies be more wisely allocated if large grants for long periods were made to universities? One comment was that each member of the university committee on grants might be in the position of voting grants to himself. So the claimed advantage of wholesaling versus retailing may not actually be achieved by allowing the university to operate as the retailer. One conferee suggested a conference where foundation leaders would exchange information on how universities operate. There were spirited criticisms of the large amount of funds available for research in the natural and physical sciences, which resulted, for example, in a deterioration in teaching. The budget of any modern large university, it was claimed, will indicate an undue stress from the standpoint of people in the social sciences, if not also the public interest, upon both teaching and research in science.

Corporate Philanthropy

Originally, both in Great Britain and in the United States, the legality of charitable or philanthropic contributions by a business firm was determined by whether they were of direct benefit to the firm. Eventually the benefit concept was supplemented when the corporation came to be regarded as just another entity in the community. Like "any other good citizen," it was argued, the corporation should be expected to accept social obligations and to support philanthropic endeavors. Contributing to the building fund for a better community hospital could be considered a benefit to the firm and a means of improving the "corporate image."

One conferee contended that, even in a widely held corporation, the proposition "what is good for the corporation is good for the community" is applicable only in the health and welfare fields. The conference was informed that a stockholder under existing law cannot require the management to submit a list of all gifts to philanthropy made directly, or through the company-sponsored foundation. The revelation by the corporation of all of its expenditures during the year that are classed as "contributions" under the federal income tax law would omit the support which corporations give to all manner of philanthropic endeavors charged to business expense. Another omission is the paid time of corporation executives and personnel given freely to support the activities of Community Chests, United Funds, and all manner of philanthropic campaigns. If as little as 0.03 per cent of the paid time of officers and employees were devoted to philanthropic endeavors, this item alone would equal 10 per cent of the amount of the contributions listed by corporations.

Some conferees disputed the right of a corporation organized for profit to give away the funds of the shareholders, that is, to impose a "tax" for philanthropy. One of the reasons, however, why corporations support philanthropic endeavors is that their employees wish them to do so. Roughly one-third of corporate giving is for philanthropy of the Community Chest type. In the past decade corporations have become more interested in giving for educational purposes. There is a noticeable tendency in corporation giving to follow the line of least resistance, giving only to the organizations listed by the Internal Revenue Service as tax-exempt institutions of a philanthropic and charitable, scientific, or educational nature.

COMPANY-SPONSORED FOUNDATIONS

The following appeared to be the most significant statements on this subject:

In order to minimize successful stockholder suits, a majority of the board members of the company-sponsored foundation should be, according to the lawyers present, company directors.

The company foundation in the last ten years has freed the corporation to some extent from supporting the pet projects of large customers, formerly an important influence in the allocation of gifts.

There are some indications that the company-sponsored foundation is more likely to employ consultants in the allocation of funds than would the company itself.

The company-sponsored foundation could stabilize the amount of corporate giving in high and low profit years.

The Value of Free Services

The conference gave some attention to the question of the imputed values of free services. Consider the housewives who devote time to gathering funds for national health agencies, local hospitals, churches, and Community Chest drives. Should an imputed value for these services, as well as the paid time of corporation executives and other personnel that is devoted to philanthropic campaigns, be added to the total economic cost of philanthropy in the United States? The imputed value of the free services—not the paid time—would constitute an appreciable addition to national income and gross national product. The principal objection was to any imputed charge to philanthropy for the unpaid leisure time a man spends attending church meetings or engaging in other philanthropic endeavors. Granting that the privilege of making a socially significant contribution of one's unpaid time to the community may be a *quid pro quo,* such massive imputations of value or cost would seem to destroy the whole concept of leisure time for 45,000,000 persons and the freedom of the individual to use that time as he sees fit. Economic Man would become so overpowering that other aspects of human life would be eliminated. Apparently most of the conferees deemed it much wiser not to try to impute values for these free services, even those that might have been purchased if they had not been given. (One enthusiastic do-it-yourself conferee, however, insisted that his homemade furniture was a tiny addition to GNP.)

Fund Raising and Private Giving

Regulatory measures other than the issuance of police-type permits are not evident in many of our cities. Some cities attempt to prohibit personal solicitation of funds. Others, notably Los Angeles, have strong regulatory commissions to which persons or organizations reveal certain facts about their organization before a license will be issued to solicit funds. In New York State, there is an SEC-type agency with which organizations are required to file before they begin fund-raising activities. In general, these regulatory bodies are concerned with fund-raising techniques, the integrity of the bookkeeping, and the accuracy of financial statements issued by the fund-raising agency. Apparently, there is more success in the area of "techniques" than in the other two areas. The most important national private evaluating agency is the National Information Bureau. The Community Chest and the United Fund exercise important regulatory functions with respect to organizations that wish to participate as members. Mention should be made, of course, of the mail fraud laws and the screening of fund-raising appeals by local and national newspapers, radio, and television. Also during World War II the National War Fund consolidated and regulated appeals of agencies collecting war relief funds.

The need for some mechanism (other than information returns or tax schedules) for evaluation of appeals to the public for funds was discussed. None was suggested for the field of education because of the strong accrediting associations which had been established and the competition among schools. The distribution of funds available for the voluntary national health agencies, however, is certainly not proportional to the number of deaths resulting annually from the diseases which are the special targets of these agencies. There does seem to be a need for a policy, which one conferee labeled a "death policy," on which to base judgment about the distribution of funds among disease categories, whether they are public funds, such as those of the National Institutes of Health, or the funds of voluntary health agencies. Or should a "death policy" be expanded into a "death and disability" policy? The relative prospects of a break-through in a particular disease seem too debatable to form a guide.

Motives for Giving

It was recognized that a great deal of pressure is exerted to persuade people to give to philanthropic endeavors. Certainly it was made clear again and again at the conference that voluntarism is a poor test for identifying philanthropy because much giving is really an exaction from individuals under pressure—even extreme pressure.

A young business executive counts it a feather in his cap to be associated with some worthwhile endeavor in the community; more likely than not, the boss allows him time off to engage in these activities. A labor leader's contribution, however, must often come during his leisure time; organized labor favors government programs instead of private philanthropy in so many of these areas.

Some of the national voluntary health agencies have made a number of studies on motivations for giving, but these studies have not been made generally available to the public. Evidently a considerable number are devoted to why an individual gives to one national health agency instead of another—an aspect of competition. Attitudes toward transfers of services to relatives outside the immediate family, broadened the discussion of giving. The motives for giving, aside from the pressures exercised by other members of the group, other members of the community, or by national advertising appeals, are extremely complex but still include the following: pity, neighborhood pride, personal prestige, the social and cultural tradition of the family, ethics, and religion.

Market Place Factors

The dividing line between market and nonmarket activities was drawn clearly. The receipt by a hospital of payments from private patients either directly or through their voluntary health insurance is an example of the private market mechanism operating in a field identified historically with philanthropy. The payment made by patients or by their insurance companies is clearly not philanthropy, but the development of mechanisms to facilitate such payments has had an effect on the development of philanthropy. It was in this connection that the discussion of market and nonmarket activities arose.

During several of the sessions, it was suggested that the subject of philanthropy could be approached from the standpoint of the imperfections of the market mechanism. Everyone could look forward to retirement without any reasonable expectation of being an object of public or private charity if, during his working life, he accumulated a sufficient pension financed in whole or in part by his employer; or if he had enough savings or enough life insurance. A sufficient amount of "permanent" life insurance for a person ending his working years of life would enable him to pay all the costs of his last illness; this is one of the reasons why people buy life insurance and continue to pay premiums. Indeed, life insurance may be the best insurance against the costs of the last illness or accident. The loan value of permanent life insurance is available in critical periods. Similar purposes could be served by the accumulation of savings and loan association shares, deposits in a savings bank, stocks and bonds, real estate, or farm land. Certainly the market-place provision for old age or for the inevitable rainy days which, if not adequate, might lead to a demand or a need for philanthropic assistance can be expanded through the process of savings or insurance. Stated another way, philanthropy may be said to be a result of the imperfections of the market place as it actually operates in human life.

The development of voluntary health insurance, particularly since 1935, illustrates this relationship between philanthropy and the market place in another fashion. Increasingly, the prepayment is becoming a part of the fringe benefits of many employees.

This portion of the discussion also included some attention to the so-called medical service entrepreneurs or merchants who are providing an increasing amount of medical or hospital services, or both, usually financed by a prepayment plan. The medical service merchant buys, so to speak, at wholesale, employs physicians and paramedical personnel, offers a wide variety of services, and retails it (furnishes the service) over the counter for cash or insurance. (Insurance organizations, of course, are not merchants in this sense; they finance but do not furnish such services as, for example, an appendectomy.) These medical services merchants are entering the field of medical care apparently on the grounds that they can do the job more efficiently. In some metropolitan centers they are becoming an important part of the market mechanism for the delivery of medical and hospital services. Many of them own hospitals as well as clinics. The medical service merchant was viewed merely as another market variant in the long development sketched here of the declining role of philanthropy in the hospital and, possibly, medical service field. The extent of philanthropy involved in their services was discussed but not estimated.

When is research an activity which belongs in the field of philanthropy and how can this research be separated from the entire universe of research activities in the United States? No hard and fast answer was found to this basic question. An illustration of philanthropic research would be that provided by a chemical company making a research grant to a university for the chemistry department, with no instructions as to the types and kinds of chemical research which could be conducted under such a grant.

Areas of Philanthropic Neglect

The conference was concerned with a number of areas in which giving seemed to be deficient—the theater, art, music, museums, and certain urban problems. These fields of activity have usually required support. The reasons for this apparent neglect were sought.

A number of nostalgic references were made to earlier centuries in which the patron supported the artist. Apparently the theory developed then that artists must be half starved to produce creative art. This notion was vigorously opposed by several of the conferees who challenged foundations to give lifetime grants to artists. One of the fundamental problems in increasing philanthropic support of the arts lies in their very nature; in this area we are likely to give honorary degrees for criticism rather than for creativity.

What kind of cultural activities in our large cities should be given more encouragement by private and public philanthropy? For music, the problem appears to spring from a limited concept, particularly in the public schools. Music should be treated as an intellectual discipline as well as an emotionally disciplined experience; either alone has limited philanthropic appeal. The mass production and mass use of hi-fidelity sets and excellent records, however, may actually be improving the appreciation of music in the United States more than is realized by persons who count the number of people who listen to good music in concert halls. The theater was believed to be in a worse state than music or any of the other fine arts. A high proportion of the members of Actors' Equity are unemployed. Could a national arts council restore the climate of culture and dignity of some of the types and kinds of TV programs which the people of the United States are expected to hear and watch? The independent educational television stations have had great financial difficulties in most cities. Considerable success has been achieved through the efforts of private foundations and other philanthropic institutions to bring traveling libraries to the smaller communities. This has also become a function of the state educational system in many states.

It is an anomaly that the federal government can send plays abroad but does not send plays throughout the United States. In Russia the government supports and controls the theater; informed conferees stated that, with some exceptions, the Russian theater experiment had produced creative art. Most of the large Swedish cities have their own opera houses and theatrical companies which are governmentally sponsored and subsidized. The tradition of royalty supporting the artist is a factor in Europe; in the United States, our democracy has no such tradition. Government aid to museums was not criticized by any of the conferees but government support of the theater was viewed with grave misgivings; and even support of music was mildly questioned. Subsidies for the construction of arts centers might encounter less objection, even during the cold war.

Some of the questions on culture incompletely answered by the conference which may be of value to the student of the problems of philanthropy were: Is there a need for community repertory theaters? Should foundations buy prime television time continuously for cultural programs? Should more city centers for operas, such as the one in New Orleans, be financed by grants? Should government subsidization of cultural television programs be undertaken? Should the Federal Communications Commission be given whatever authority it needs to compel commercial television stations to measure up to a higher cultural standard?

The conference turned its attention to several urban problems particularly that of the Negro; and reviewed the status of philanthropic endeavors in this field. What can philanthropy do to help solve the very difficult problems of the Negro in our large cities, particularly the young Negro? (The problem in rural areas was not discussed.) The traditional general measures such as the maintenance of a health and welfare program, various types of social planning, family counseling, etc., were reviewed. The migration to the city by the Negro poses problems that are, of course, different from those of earlier migrations. For example, the Irish were eager to own property and the Italians and Jews were ambitious to have their children educated. The problems of the Negro are more intense. The Julius Rosenwald Fund has been liquidated. Is there a need for another Rosenwald foundation? Should a special effort be made to instruct Negroes about the dangers of going into debt? Stress was laid on the point that within the Negro community itself those Negroes who attempt to assert leadership are often discouraged from doing so. One of the conferees observed that as the Negro's economic status rises he does not tend to contribute more to the support of the members of his community.

Public Policy and Philanthropy

The changing relationship between government, welfare, and philanthropy was one of the liveliest and most controversial subjects treated at this conference on philanthropy. (If Barzun[1] had been present, I doubt that he would have continued to consider philanthropy one of the three enemies of the Intellect.) The discussion of this changing relationship was spread over several sessions, and certainly provided some sharp challenges and observations on public policy and historical trends, as well as on the current situation.

In the approach to public policy it was noted that private philanthropic organizations often carry out some functions which might be called "state" functions in addition to the purely private ones. Likewise, it is not completely fair to think of their private activities as being wholly "privately financed" when discussing their tax position and other matters of public policy. The determination of the final resting place of the burden of taxes created by certain exemptions for philanthropic organizations and their donors was noted by the conference as a subject that needed a great deal more attention than it had received. With highly progressive rates of income taxation, the government has in effect chosen or committed itself to match private contributions on the basis of the effective marginal rate of tax for the contributor. The government hence has to dip into high incomes with a sieve, since the high income taxpayer obviously has a lower "net cost of giving" than does the low income taxpayer. An examination of giving to philanthropic endeavors by the very high income receivers indicates, however, that full "advantage" is not taken, for example, of the nine to one ratio by persons in the 90 per cent tax bracket. It was contended that nine parts of his gifts are really income taxes not levied and only one part would have been left as after-tax income. On the other hand, some of the expenditures of private philanthropic agencies reduce the need for government expenditures and revenues.

A conferee contended that one of the reasons why the wealthy did not seem to give as much as their incomes would indicate they should (and did not seem to realize the nine to one advantage that they had in giving) was due to the fact that some of the new or only temporarily wealthy are included in the annual statistics. In a metropolitan com-

[1] In *The House of Intellect* (New York, 1959), Jacques Barzun describes the three enemies of the intellect: art, science, and philanthropy; he also devotes Chapter Four to the "Folklore of Philanthropy."

munity it is quite possible for them, especially those lacking religious affiliations, to remain relatively isolated and "anonymously wealthy."

In addition to freedom from federal tax on their current income, philanthropic organizations enjoy the distinction of having gifts to them legally deductible from the taxable income of the donor up to 20 per cent or, for some gifts, 30 per cent of his income. (The state income tax laws provide a variety of deductions.) On the other hand, charitable bequests (made by wills) are free from federal tax in any amount provided the purpose is charitable, educational, scientific, religious. Other western countries have more limited systems of special privilege for philanthropic institutions.

It was observed that any potential tendency for favorable tax treatment in the aggregate to create centers of power by philanthropic institutions would be found in the areas of religion and education, and in foundations. The extensive property holdings of some of the churches, one conferee contended, is eroding the property tax base in certain areas.

Local administration of welfare programs has persisted but with an increasing portion of state and federal financing. Provision of funds by the federal government has brought with it a degree of standardization and control; but a large measure of control is still exercised through the instrumentalities of the various states. The entrance of the federal government into the fields formerly largely preempted by the local and state governments and private philanthropy has undoubtedly resulted in raising the amount of the benefits, standards of training of personnel, clarification of eligibility requirements, and the right of confidential records being accorded to welfare recipients. (One conferee briefly outlined his alternative proposal of *social budgeting* which had first been presented under that label in 1937.)

From some points of view the largest public assistance and welfare program in the United States is the veterans' program ($5 billion a year). It is the oldest and largest federal aid program. Its inclusion as philanthropy was not uniformly acceptable to all of the conferees. One thought that the veterans' program should be viewed as an expression of gratitude by the people of the nation for the services rendered by veterans. Others thought that the entire veterans' program had to be considered a form of public charity.

One problem for the conference was to decide whether, for example, old age assistance when provided under a federal-state program is philanthropy, although every conferee would admit that provision for the old had been one of the primary objects of philanthropy for centuries.

The future expansion of social security will cast a shadow, a long shadow over the future of public philanthropy (or government welfare, or public and private welfare, or whatever it may come to be called). It may be now, or later may become, the largest item in philanthropy. Certainly there are transfer payments from the rich and poor young to rich and poor old in the present social security program. Whether one calls this public philanthropy or social charity (as was apparently the implication of the encyclical of Pope John XXIII issued from Rome on May 15, 1961) or modern substitutes for private philanthropy is a question of terminology. Whatever the choice of nomenclature, it was clear that the conferees could not possibly discuss philanthropy without considering the impact of some of these governmental welfare programs. They involve a very large flow of funds. The impact on private philanthropy has been extensive; for example, private agencies dealing with the blind are no longer concerned with poor relief for the blind.

In the summer of 1961, when this conference was held, no one could be unaware of the large problem of foreign aid in the world today and its possible future developments. But the conference was also concerned with terms; and the question of terms here was whether helping the starving people of foreign countries through governmental plans was properly designated "public philanthropy" when helping the starving people of foreign countries through private agencies is and always has been unquestionably within the scope of philanthropy. The maintenance of the church missionaries in Africa and in other sections of the world during this period of nationalism, and in the face of the attempts of communists to spread antireligious propaganda throughout the world is truly remarkable. It brings up the question of including or not including foreign aid in the form of, for example, technical assistance within the broad concept of philanthropy. Certainly a portion of the foreign aid of recent years has been of a type which resembles the nonpreaching activities of our foreign missionaries for more than 100 years. No conferee contended that every dollar of foreign aid was money thrown away foolishly, although many of our citizens apparently hold that view. These questions about foreign aid in relation to a broad concept of philanthropy are not easy. During World War I when Herbert Hoover led the great humanitarian effort to help feed the people of Belgium and a small sector of northern France, more than 90 per cent of the funds used were of public (governmental) origin rather than private. Does that mean that in the light of history we should exclude the vast and successful attempt to feed those starving people as being outside of the pale of philanthropy? Some of the conferees said no, others yes. There seemed to be agreement among the conferees only on the proposition that there was a charitable element in part or most of our foreign aid operations, but that this was mixed in with national interest and the two were, are, and doubtless will continue to be difficult to separate. The amount of our foreign aid is becoming very large indeed and attempts should be made to place it in the right position in our national accounts.

Doubtless the development of a completely satisfactory nomenclature for such a dynamic subject as philanthropy in an affluent society must await the clarification of some of the concepts in the growing fields of public welfare and foreign aid. Again, philanthropy is literally "love of mankind." It involves concepts of social justice and social charity. In a very dynamic period it is difficult to circumscribe the flow of funds into activities that inherently possess no clearly discernible economic boundaries. This conference on philanthropy explored but did not locate those boundaries.

The Poor Law Revisited

WILLARD L. THORP
The Merrill Center for Economics and Amherst University

IT MIGHT be argued that philanthropy has no place in economics—that it consists of "noneconomic" acts which should more properly be studied by other disciplines. But these acts are substantive and substantial, and have reason to be of interest to the economist. They affect the allocation of scarce resources, the distribution of income, and the flow of funds through the public sector. Philanthropy presents its claims on the assets of the individual, the business enterprise, and the government. In turn it provides recipients selected on a wide variety of bases with a kind of unearned income which might be charged against the economy as an external cost in the form of social overhead. Philanthropy does not fit into the traditional economic production and income distribution model.

On its institutional side, philanthropy has developed rapidly expanding organizational forms whose handling of assets, income, and expenditures does not correspond to the theory of the business firm with its cost and revenue functions. Nor, except for public agencies themselves, can the behavior of philanthropic enterprises be explained by the principles which relate to expenditures and revenues in the public economy.

To some extent there is a precedent for economists to consider these matters. Adam Smith saw the operation of the English Poor

NOTE: This paper, stimulated by the discussions at the Merrill Center concerning philanthropy, is not a summary of the conference, but represents one participant's reaction to that stimulant some six months later. In refreshing his recollection, the author has relied heavily upon notes made at the time by Edward J. Kane of Princeton University and the acute comments of his wife, Clarice Brows Thorp.

Law as interfering with labor mobility. Malthus criticized it much more strongly as an ineffective palliative. Sismondi argued for putting all responsibility for the workers' illness and old age on the employer in order to make certain that it would be carried as a labor cost and not a public charge. John Stuart Mill, on the other hand, was against patriarchal and paternalistic arrangements whereby the poor relied on their superiors "to do all that is necessary to ensure their being, in return for labour and attachment, properly fed, clothed, housed, spiritually edified and innocently amused." [1] He was in favor of rugged individualism even as to amusement and, where public charity was necessary, held that it should be so limited as to assure a built-in motive for the individual to seek an alternative, perhaps even by seeking employment. Alfred Marshall [2] carried on the classical tradition by including the "injudicious poor law" among the causes which, early in the nineteenth century, brought "the working classes into the greatest misery they have ever suffered." He also argued that the principle "that the State should take account only of destitution and not at all of merit" reduces savings, to the extent that they become less essential in providing for an individual's future.

Classical economists, then, tended to regard charity and philanthropy primarily as interferences with proper economic motivation, providing rewards for economic dereliction. This point of view is often expressed today in the public debates concerning domestic and foreign government aid. However, one finds surprisingly little about philanthropy in current professional economic literature. To be sure, a brief description of "social security" through government programs appears in most elementary economic textbooks, and various aspects of such programs have been examined from time to time. Economists have recently begun to pay some attention to the economics of education and of health. And the increased assumption of "welfare" burdens by the state encourages the everlasting debate over the proper boundary between the private and public sector.

The Philanthropic Revolution

As soon as one begins to explore this area, it becomes apparent that it is of substantial economic importance and that major changes are

[1] John Stuart Mill, *Principles of Political Economy,* Book IV, Chapter VII, Section 1.

[2] Alfred Marshall, *Principles of Economics,* Book IV, Chapter IV, Section 2, and Book IV, Chapter VII, Section 4.

taking place. It is not merely a set of arrangements for taking care of paupers and unfortunates, but it reaches into strategic areas such as education, research, and foreign relations. The government is now active on a large scale in many of the fields, such as old age and disability, traditionally (except for pauper cases) occupied by the family or the private agency. In research, the government also has become a prime mover, though national drives to collect funds from individuals, particularly for projects involving medical research, have reappeared; they were discouraged earlier by the effort to consolidate all appeals in annual Community Chest and United Fund drives.

The corporation as donor and the rapidly growing foundation represent fairly recent entrants into the field whose importance is mounting rapidly. Private agencies have moved into the area of family adjustment problems and the foreign missionary is now overshadowed by new types of private and government foreign aid projects. On the other hand, the consumer is now paying for a larger share of his hospital and medical care. In total, what is probably a growing amount of resources is being allocated in a shifting pattern through changing institutional arrangements.

It is perhaps worth noting that these changes have themselves raised questions about the use of the term "philanthropy." The concept always has been more operational than logical. The effort to distinguish according to motive runs into all the complications of multiple causation and the hedonistic calculus. Areas and functions do not provide a clear basis for distinction. Philanthropy in common parlance is broader than charity, since it includes such activities as support of education, research, and cultural activities. One can question the extent to which support of education and, even more, of research belongs under the heading of philanthropy. What distinctions, if any, should be made as to support of public schools, parochial schools, private colleges, and state universities? To be sure, public charity has always been recognized, but how deal with publicly operated social security (financed in part by the beneficiaries), research supported by Defense Department funds, state government support to universities, and foreign assistance, to none of which are the taxpayers voluntary contributors? Perhaps it is best to regard this as another dimension of the "mixed economy," where flexibility and change are replacing firm and fixed parameters and perimeters.

To some extent, this philanthropic revolution is a reflection of changes in the nature of modern living, of shifting objectives in our social values, and of a new relationship now generally accepted between the government and the individual. Higher incomes more widely distributed have alleviated the general problem of poverty so that less energy goes today into the ancient and honorable practice of distributing Thanksgiving baskets to the hungry and more into the rising problem of poverty of symphony orchestras and creative artists. An increasing proportion of the eligible age group is demanding higher education but the higher income levels have not kept down an increased demand for scholarships. Another new set of problems arises from increased urbanization, particularly when it involves large national or racial groups. The philanthropic revolution is also a reflection of new and needed additions to knowledge. New developments in sociology and psychiatry have suggested ways of dealing with problems of maladjustment. And new technology needs research both in development and application—as in the case of the use of television in education.

Most important as a force for change in the central core of philanthropic activity has been the acceptance of general social responsibility for the protection of the individual against economic want resulting from old age, unemployment, disability, and other misfortunes. Since the mid-thirties, government programs have rapidly expanded. They have been "assurance" rather than "insurance," if the first is taken to mean the provision of protection and the latter to mean an actuarial distribution of risk. However labeled, government programs have come to occupy a large part of the area formerly covered by the family and the private agency.

Individual Giving

There are innumerable questions here which should challenge an economist. First, consider microeconomic matters. What do we know about the process of donation? How can one rationalize in general terms the behavior of the foundation or the corporation or even the individual donor? Perhaps the individual has some means of measuring his own satisfactions so that he can compare the pleasure of obtaining a receipted statement for his contribution to the American Red Cross with the pleasure of possessing a new pair of shoes, as easily as he can compare the latter with some additions to his library. But if he does so compare, he must plug in to his personal computer all the variables of social pressures, habit, emotional appeal, misinformation, and social and individual scales of values.

Some information is available about individual giving. Perhaps the most startling is that on 46 per cent of the tax returns reporting annual incomes in excess of $250,000, deductions for contributions were less than 2 per cent of income. There are various explanations of this phenomenon beyond that of individual attitude—that many individuals have highly unstable incomes, that some high income recipients succeed in concealing the fact from all solicitors, and that there are wealthy migrants who are not members of any "community." Similar factors also may affect the behavior of lower income groups. At any rate, it seems clear that one cannot easily assume the existence of a relatively stable or relatively simple function called the "propensity to give." One can readily list elements which must bear on choice and rejection but little study has been made of their relative significance. It can be said that the current trend in personal giving seems to be less in the direction of redistributing income and more toward the support of professional activities and provision for collective wants.

In actual fact, the individual donor is poorly equipped to make a rational selection among the appeals which he receives. He is to some degree protected from rackets by the Treasury's selection of agencies, contributions to which are eligible for tax deduction. In some areas there are local regulations concerning solicitation. Perhaps there ought to be a philanthropy guide for the average man. Most contributors would like to know what proportion of the funds given reaches the alleged objective, what is the importance of the problem and the potential for achievement, and how efficient is the operation. While such ideal comparisons are obviously impossible, it may be that more can be done to help the giver in making his allocations. If the objective is "social climbing," expert advisors are available. The Community Chest is a device for allocation among applicants. But individual donors who make their own choices have little objective information on which they can rely. To the extent that donations are made by corporations, foundations, and government agencies, it can be assumed that they are likely to rely upon staff members who are experienced in the screening process.

Up to this point, the discussion has been in terms of material contributions without noting that there are donors who give services where no economic record is made. Volunteer services range all the way from considerable personal sacrifice to calculated investment. Little seems to be known about this part of the philanthropic process. Even if it were decided to recognize volunteer services by imputation, the problem of what valuation to impute would provide another hurdle. How value the services of the company vice-president who heads the local drive—especially since part of his activity may be on company time (and with its blessing); or the housewife who helps in the hospital on Tuesdays and plays bridge on other days. Volunteer work is an important factor affecting the broad flow of philanthropic activity. But has it a reverse income elasticity, so that it will fall as incomes rise? Is it a substitute for or a stimulant to cash contributions? It is worth noting that any change in the extent of volunteer activity is almost certain to affect the apparent dollar cost of these services.

It would be helpful to know more about the income elasticity of individual giving. The subelasticities appear to vary with age and income—lower income and older groups tend to give relatively more to religious institutions, for example. There also appears to be a degree of cyclical variation, particularly since certain of the needs are clearly reflections of variations in business conditions. But the most basic problem is the relationship between rising incomes and philanthropic contributions. This is no easy matter to assess, particularly in view of the tax angles and the increased activity of government in the field. Thus one cannot easily explain the past trend or extrapolate into the future.

Presumably, detailed scrutiny of the behavior of the individual donor can be avoided, in the manner to which economists are accustomed, by taking spender choice for granted and leaving most of the basic problem of how personal priorities are established to other disciplines. But the foundation, the corporation, the nonprofit philanthropic agency, and the government are man-made entities which operate within man-made rules. At least the economist should be concerned with the rules, so far as they exist, and with their absence if they do not exist. He has some obligations to consider how, and possibly even how well or badly, the presumed functions of these agencies are being performed in the philanthropic area (however that is defined) and what future developments are likely to be.

The Corporation as Donor

The corporation case has many interesting facets. Presumably, a corporation is operated by management in the interest of the stockholders. Its objective is profit maximization. Under such a simple proposition, there seems to be no place for philanthropy in the literal sense. But perhaps in its own interest the corporation can contribute to what would be regarded as charitable purposes: it needs the good will of the police so it contributes to their welfare association; it salvages employee time if a competent local hospital is near, etc. Such contributions may qualify as costs of doing business and may be treated as such by that final taxonomic authority, the Commissioner of Internal Revenue.

Where is the line to be drawn between costs and philanthropy? A corporation has a general interest in the availability of educated personnel. Does this justify contributions to distant colleges and universities? Does it help if the corporation limits its contributions to institutions which have provided at least one graduate for its payroll? Or, to push the line even further, since the private corporation would be destroyed if there were a communist takeover in the United States, is it performing a service to its stockholders if it supports general economic education or various anticommunist organizations?

Until relatively recently, the idea that a corporation might make contributions other than those clearly in its own interest was open to serious legal question. However, various state laws have been enacted which protect boards of directors from stockholder action, and the federal corporation income tax permits a deduction of philanthropic contributions up to 5 per cent of corporate income. Obviously, this tax deduction acts as a multiplier and provides a considerable incentive, as indicated by the fact that corporate contributions increased substantially during the last year of the high corporate excess profits tax. The stockholders play very little part in this matter, either by approval expressed at the annual meeting or by the indirect controls of full and detailed disclosure.

One can never tell when publicity will break out concerning this or that corporate action, and the corporation must keep not only its stockholders in mind but also its employees and customers. All groups can be disturbed by allegations of scandal and even by the mere accusation of impropriety. As a form of protection from just this sort of thing, corporations and corporate foundations seldom give grants to individuals, but contribute to institutions, projects, and causes. Except for support to higher education, the tendency seems to be to focus on grants for services in communities in which the corporation operates and to channel them through noncontroversial agencies which would presumably be approved by the overwhelming majority of the stockholders. (Such a guide tends to rule out contributions to sectarian religious organizations.)

Corporate activity in connection with philanthropy can be viewed as diminishing the extent of voluntarism in private giving. The direct contribution of corporation funds is hardly a voluntary act by the stockholders, and this together with payroll deduction plans is providing an increasingly large proportion of Community Chest and United Fund collections. In some cases, corporate contributions (plus those treated as costs) are large in size and their allocation has considerable social significance. There is little information concerning the actual disposition of these funds, but under the circumstances there is reason to expect that they are used to support conservative and "safe" activities.

It seems likely that the amount of corporation giving will increase and its scope will broaden. Greater support may be anticipated for cultural activities and research in those areas in the humanities and social science not under the aegis of the National Science Foundation. With the clear trend toward building a special staff for screening applications and appeals, a professional group is becoming established which will have an interest in the maintenance and promotion of corporate giving, and which can present possible philanthropic projects to the appropriating authorities in an effective manner.

The Foundation

The problems of the foundation take quite a different turn. Foundations are not new inventions. Both Carnegie and Rockefeller antedate World War I. However, the present scale of foundation growth is new. On the average, one hundred new foundations are formed every month and there were more than 13,000 foundations at the beginning of 1962. Most of these are small, but several very large additions are expected within the next decade. With the public becoming ever more educated to the tax and other advantages which can accrue to the founder of a foundation, such growth is not unlikely.

The foundation receives funds from some donor and then must administer them. To some extent, of course, this is merely a rechanneling of private giving, but the total probably is increased in the process. The primary requirements of this enterprise are that it must not make a profit (except that it may make a capital gain) and must give away its income. The original terms of the trust may call for dispersal of the principal over some period of time and may define broadly or narrowly the purposes to which its funds can be used.

The foundation buys "proposals" rather than "results." It finances activities whose value can perhaps never be determined. There is no analogue of the market or the voting booth to enforce any discipline upon it. The original gift may include detailed instructions to the trustees, but frequently the trustees (usually self-perpetuating) have only a general sort of welfare direction given them by the original donor. What then is their specific guide and to whom are they responsible? The answer appears to be that the trustees in such a case have an extraordinary degree of freedom to dispose of funds as they see fit without review by anyone. They may of course be sensitive to public relations and the always possible Congressional inquiry.

The larger foundations have developed staffs which screen proposals received, as well as think up projects themselves. At the other extreme are the large number of small foundations which are merely different legal forms for individual giving. These are likely to follow the donor's line of interest, often emphasizing activities in the immediate community which depend otherwise on individual gifts. However, even this process of institutionalizing contributions may have one useful result, in that it may lead to more careful consideration of alternatives. At present there seems to be little exchange of information and experience among either large or small donors but it probably is inevitable that formal kinds of exchange will develop eventually.

Strangely enough, this new form of enterprise has received very little study except through self-analysis—but there has been much of that. (The Ford Foundation began such a self-evaluation late in 1960.) We know little about the social costs of foundations (exemptions from taxes and expert time consumed, for example), the nature of their process of decision-making, their optimum size, what factors limit their activity, and what are the appropriate areas for their functioning. A few foundations are highly conspicuous but there are additional thousands, often very small, about which little has been written. Bornet's[3] study of nonprofit enterprises is the only real cross-section study which exists, even though substantial amounts of data are obtainable since the law requires annual reports to be filed and to be available for inspection.

Though it is frequently argued that full disclosure provides some form of protection, it also is argued that a greater degree of publicity or disclosure might be bad because one of the great values of this new institutional form is its freedom to experiment and innovate. While disclosure might avoid public misunderstanding and tend to encourage competition among the foundations themselves, it would seem likely to encourage conservative performance and "safe" grants. Nevertheless, the large foundations have clearly been under some

[3] Vaughn Davis Bornet, *California Social Welfare,* Englewood Cliffs, N.J., 1956.

kind of inner compulsion to report their activities in considerable detail.

There is every reason to expect substantial increases in the sums disbursed by foundations. To some extent, there has been little need to worry about misallocation in the past because of the limited scale of operation and the number of independent operators. The problems assume a different social and economic significance if one envisages something like a doubling of the foundation population in each size bracket. It is becoming increasingly clear that the larger foundations cannot act as retailers; they are finding it necessary to make their contributions in large blocks to other existing institutions. This becomes a kind of wholesaling operation, with retail distribution by the university, research agency, or professional group. While this process does tend to strengthen the already successful, it probably widens the range of projects and individuals who can obtain support.

Since there are no maximum wage laws, the foundations are free to use unusual economic inducements to draw staff persons from other areas. If the more inflated predictions are true, the expansion of foundation funds and the necessity for their expenditure may lead to an increasing number of high-level individuals being drawn away from various pursuits in order to dispense funds to those who were left behind. This may add to the forces leading to increased welfare in academic circles!

What is the test of excellence for the foundation? The ordinary business firm can be judged by its profits and if it is grossly inefficient, it will not long survive. A foundation can survive any number of bad grants; its survival depends solely on competent investment skill. Even if it is responsible enough to undertake self-evaluation, it will do so according to its own scale of values. It is not enough for a foundation to lie on the couch and listen to itself, but where can it turn for competent criticism, and what yardsticks should the critic use? Perhaps a new chapter needs to be added in the textbooks after the theory of the firm to deal with the theory of the foundation. But someone will have to construct that theory first. And when he does, he will want to give some attention to the peculiarities of the corporation-sponsored foundation which operates not from a capital fund but from occasional (often annual) corporate appropriations.

Government as Donor

One of the main arguments in support of corporation and foundation giving is that this aids in the preservation of our pluralistic society, i.e., it reduces the function of government in that society. There is no question but that among the greatest changes in recent years in the area of philanthropy has been the extent to which the government has expanded its "welfare" activities. In large part, this is a substitution of government-given assurances through formal rules for long-established but uncertain private activities. As a result, voluntary agencies are almost completely out of the "relief" business; they have mostly redirected their activities and have become therapeutic agencies, family and youth agencies, agencies for the blind, and the like.

Social scientists have paid much more attention to government entry into the field than to private activity. In part this is because there is substantial documentation and public debate. Because the problems are more familiar, they are here given little attention despite their scale and scope. Among the notable issues is that of the division of function among federal, state, and local levels. Local administration of programs has persisted despite an increasing portion of federal finance and considerable federal standardization of operations in such matters as eligibility requirements, quality of personnel, and rights accorded welfare recipients.

The Recipients of Aid

So far the discussion has dealt primarily with the donors. A new set of behavioral problems are created for the recipients of aid. Here we must distinguish between a possible intermediate recipient, that is, an agency which is seeking support, and the ultimate recipient. As a general proposition, it can be said that a large part of government aid goes directly to the ultimate recipient. Social security payments would be a clear case and aid to hospitals and universities may be regarded as aid to the final beneficiary. Private donors are likely to make their contributions to organizations, since that is the way to achieve tax deductions.

However, the picture is not quite so clear as it appears above. The interplay of private agency and government has taken various forms. To some extent, welfare needs have developed their own self-supporting institutions: private pension plans; income, disability, and retirement insurance; and medical plans. And even when the government has entered a field, it may still deal with the problem by contributing to the current operating costs of the services of private agencies. Such arrangements preserve the identity of the voluntary agency providing the service but may restrict its area of activity, or limit its freedom to innovate. Government support seems necessary where private givers are reluctant to contribute, possibly because the problem is unpopular (family desertion or racial discrimination) or because there is skepticism as to the effectiveness of social work techniques.

Perhaps the largest group of ultimate recipients are those who receive government aid through various welfare and social security programs. This process has an effect both upon the recipient and upon his confreres. The possible undermining of individual ambition has long been discussed in connection with social security provisions. Today, opponents of some form of subsidized medical care argue that added public support will place undue burdens on the medical profession. In the academic world, considerable attention has been paid to the possible conflict between those in the same university engaged in generously supported research and those who are teaching or working on problems which are less appealing to grantors. And sometimes internal conflicts are created for those who receive grants. Economists, for example, appear to have exaggerated notions as to the speed and effectiveness with which they can complete a research project. The receipt of a grant and failure to hold to the schedule set out in the application lead to guilt feelings. For most economists who appear to have production potentials, the summer reading period has disappeared.

Perhaps the most immediate problem is that of how relations can be most efficiently and expeditiously established between donor and grantee. The initiative may come from either side—a foundation may be seeking a man to carry out some project which it is eager to sponsor or a man with a project may be seeking financial support. The problem is similar to that of college entrance, where the process of matching is so wasteful, nerve-racking, and long-drawn-out. But applicants for grants are busy people who cannot, like the college-admission seeker, visit a number of foundations and study their catalogs. Like any market or employment operation, better information concerning availabilities and alternatives might help. How much time and energy is exhausted under present conditions would be difficult even to guess.

One great change has taken place in recent years in the relationship between grantor and grantee. In the twenties it was regarded as quite improper for a teacher to receive assistance from a business enterprise and even to use pamphlets and other teaching material from business sources. Today there is no longer the automatic suspicion of tainted money and a sell-out. Possibly the academic world has more confidence in its own morality, perhaps business is less demanding; certainly there is less feeling of inevitable antagonism between the two. Nevertheless, the donee still may have his doubts about the attitude of some interested donor, and may look to the more "objective" foundation to support him with a minimum of interference. Nevertheless, the problem remains because even the process of selection is a kind of interference by those who hold the purse strings.

There are additional complications. One can never know how many proposals are developed for personal reasons, such as prestige, or the free trip, or because of institutional pressures. Applications are inevitably shaped to achieve their purpose. If the applicant is not able to strike an immediate match, he may accept suggestions for alterations—or he may exhaust himself in the search for a sponsor. Perhaps this disorderly process may produce the high spots in any random distribution but it has unfortunate aspects of waste. It is hard to regard it as an efficient method of balancing resources against short- and long-run needs.

Another group needs some mention—the workers in the various philanthropic service agencies. To some extent they find themselves in a special category. The largest employers of such workers, the nation's hospitals, have argued that unless they are exempt from labor legislation they could not continue to hire the relatively "unemployable." Religious organizations have invoked the church-state rubric. And the situation of the paid employee is affected by the numbers of voluntary workers whose presence influences wage levels, working conditions, and discipline.

Sources of Funds

From the point of view of the over-all use of resources, the macroeconomic considerations, there are also a number of important problems which should be explored. Traditional economic processes operate in some sectors of the philanthropic area. The economics of hospitalization and medical care have been transformed by the new institutions such as Blue Cross and Blue Shield. This development has brought about a much closer balance of costs and payments and reduced the part of the operating costs which depends on philanthropy. Similarly, increased tuitions in various educational institutions have been of importance. Growth in the use of commercial loans for education and educational institutions, hospitalization and surgical insurance schemes, and private pension plans provide ample illustrations of the extent of adaptation that has occurred. Nevertheless, for hospitals and educational institutions, the provision of new capital requirements still largely depends on government or philanthropic aid. (This situation is obscured by the development of federal government action as a guarantor for certain capital loans.)

One of the interesting phases of the over-all distribution of resources is the great assist given to philanthropy by the government through tax measures. The donor is encouraged to make contributions to religious, charitable, and educational organizations by an allowance of tax deductions which may reach 30 per cent of adjusted gross income. In addition, by giving capital assets instead of money, a donor can realize a capital gain without becoming subject to the usual capital gains tax. And charitable bequests in any amount are fully exempt from the estate tax. (State inheritance laws vary on this point.)

The organization itself is exempted from local taxation on its property and, as a nonprofit enterprise, from any tax on its income. In most states, it enjoys another special privilege—immunity from tort liability for the acts of its employees. There are other special exemptions, such as the exemption from the transportation tax for persons traveling on university business. To what extent would these organizations survive without this help? Is this a true separation of the state and religious establishment? What about the burden on local taxpayers in a community where much property is exempt? Special notice should be taken of the foundation in this respect, since undoubtedly much of the motivation for transferring personal assets to a foundation arises from the voracious nature of the income, capital gains, and inheritance tax structures.

In fact, under some circumstances, contributing can be profitable. Suppose a man in the 91 per cent income tax bracket holds a security now valued at $10,000 for which he paid $2,000. If he sells it and pays 25 per cent capital gains tax, he is left with $8,000 cash on hand. But if he gives the security to a charitable institution, he can deduct the full amount and thus reduce his income tax by $9,100. Not only is he better off by $1,100 but he has the credit for being a generous donor! The fact that the proportion of people itemizing their deductions rose from 50% to 70% between 1948 and 1958 can be considered an indication that the process of deduction encourages philanthropic giving.

Neither the origins of these forms of special treatment nor their impact on the total flow of private contributions to philanthropy are at all clear. Certainly, the usual efforts to divide contributions into public and private are misleading, since that part of private gifts which is offset by a reduced tax should logically be credited to the public sector. This privileged position for philanthropy may be attributed to the social value of the objectives involved, the lack of direct reward to the donor (the tax deduction is described by one author [4] as "a sort of monetary ointment to salve the strain of charity"), the outgrowth of early common law concepts, or the constitutional dichotomy between church and state. One objection to the present situation is that the wealthy contributor has such great leverage and can, in a sense, give away other taxpayers' money at his discretion anywhere within the boundaries of the tax deduction provision. The tax inducement operates on the large donor more than on the small, and influences the beneficiaries to take the unusual position of arguing against a reduction in income tax rates or in the capital gains tax.

The Allocation of Resources

It is difficult to find what over-all forces determine the allocation of these funds. For example, why is so much money going into medical research and so little into racial problems? Any one field, of course, can be the popular area of the moment, or even the "safest" from the point of view of popular (or Congressional) criticism. Somewhere there is an ultimate limit on the expansion in any field, set by the availability of competent manpower. Competition among grantors to support research by members of some limited group can lead to more and more generous grants and possibly to the creation of unfortunate scarcities in the other areas in which those with the same competence are required. Too much promotion of a narrowly defined area can attract scarce intellects into relatively barren or overplowed fields. This is particularly true if one thinks too much in terms of projects rather than people.

Shortage of manpower is a form of control which will operate only at extremes and cannot assure the appropriate allocation of funds among such diverse claimants as medical research, museums, religious

[4] Philip E. Taylor, *Economics of Public Finance,* New York, p. 432.

bodies, family welfare agencies, university scholarships and fellowships, symphony orchestras, and nonprofit cemeteries. So far as operation within the public sector is concerned, the usual forces which play upon the political organs are there. So far as the agencies which exist on drives are concerned, one can say that the public does have something to say about allocation. But here results depend primarily upon the effectiveness of the appeal to donors, which may be more a matter of presentation than substance.

The Need for Further Study

Even to put these problems in proper perspective, much more is needed in the way of information. The National Bureau has undertaken its study in large part because of its special interest in national income measurement. To the extent that nonprofit organizations (including nonphilanthropic ones, such as labor unions and country clubs) employ individuals, pay rent, and purchase goods and services from business, they contribute to the estimates of gross national product; other disbursements, such as cash handouts, material gifts, and dues, are disregarded. The concept of transfer payments is employed for certain activities of government, business, and individuals in order that *A*'s income when transferred to and spent by *B* will not be counted twice as income and once as expenditures. These transfer payments do not appear in gross national product or national income estimates.

The statistical estimates will give a quantitative setting, but this is only a beginning. Suppose the data verify the general belief that endowments and activities of foundations, educational institutions, and church groups are growing at a rapid rate. Resulting shifts in economic strength may affect economic activity and the allocation of resources. If one counts government expenditures, it seems certain that the total will mount. Coverage tends to broaden and programs to be extended. The emphasis on the aged, the new programs for aid to distressed areas, the limited experiments in relocation and retraining, and efforts at urban planning and redevelopment—all are potential claimants for much greater resources. The private agencies also have new areas to occupy, as, for example, the hard-core problem family, the juvenile delinquent, the migrant to the city. And other areas need both government and private help—the problems of race, promotion of culture, and the city youth drop-outs from school, to list only three. Both private and public agencies are operating on an unprecedented scale in foreign countries where age-old problems appear in old and new forms.

Despite the fact that it has always been with us, there is much about philanthropy which is not known. The practitioners may be competent in their special fields—the social worker with her cases and the hospital administrator with his budget. But the broader problems of requirements, performance, cost, organizational effectiveness, and appropriate public policy are all in need of exploration. The lack of conclusions by the conferees at the Merrill Center was clear evidence of the limited knowledge which carefully selected experts could bring to bear on the questions under discussion. The need is apparent for much more research in depth, and for a continuous review of policy relating to the location and basis of responsibility in this important area.

UNION CARBIDE CORPORATION
DEC 27 1962
BUSINESS LIBRARY